THE SPICE OF LIFE

Lord Nathan.

The Spice of Life

Lord Nathan

ROGER NATHAN

MC

First published in 2003 by
The Memoir Club
Whitworth Hall
Spennymoor
County Durham

British Library Cataloguing-in-Publication data
A catalogue record for this book is available from the British Library

ISBN 1-84104-060-6

The descriptions of events, incidents and characters featured in this book are true and correct according to the recollections of the author

Printed in the UK by Biddles Ltd, Guildford and Kings Lynn

Contents

List of Illustrations

Introduction

A MEMBER OF MY FAMILY suggested to me a long time ago that I should briefly record some of the amusing and interesting events which I had experienced. Subsequently one or two friends suggested that I should write a brief memoir.

This book derives entirely from recollection – as I have never kept a diary – so there are likely to be errors and there are certainly omissions both accidental and purposely made to avoid an overlong book. In writing it I had in mind that my children may be interested as well as my close friends, but not the wider public to whom any published book may come.

It was The Memoir Club, the publishers, who advised me that it would be of interest to a wider public than my own family and close friends and that is the reason for its publication. I hope that those who read it may find it amusing and of interest and that they will forgive the errors and omissions which they will undoubtedly find.

I was associated either as a member or chairman with a large number of voluntary organisations, which I found stimulating, particularly if they were new or had no longstanding tradition or history. It was then possible to try to imprint one's own ideas upon it. I have felt that about five years is the appropriate time to hold such office, as this is generally long enough to give what one has to offer and it is then right to make way for others to do the same. I believe many involved in such organisations often remain in office for too long. That is one reason why I found myself associated with so many different organisations over the years to all of whom I am most grateful for the opportunity to embark on new ventures.

Of course throughout my active life legal practice was the centre of activity and I am grateful for the support and understanding of my

Partners in accepting that with a wide range of interests and activity within it a burden of providing specialist expertise was often laid upon them. I am also grateful for their tolerance of much activity outside the practice, which inevitably cast additional work on them.

If any of them should read this book I hope they will have a good laugh at some of the events of which they well knew – and some of which they did not!

I dedicate this book to my children and their children in the hope that in their lives and careers they will have as much fun as I have had.

CHAPTER I

The Early Years

I DO NOT KNOW when my parents bought 15 Lansdowne Road where I spent my earliest years – nor do I remember it well. It was a family house in the Victorian style and there was a garden for use in common by residents in the road. I do remember there were tortoises in the garden and that there was a lot of crazy paving on the paths. I remember well a large room on perhaps the second floor where in 1928 I was taken ill with diphtheria, which in those days was a very serious illness. Sir William Wilcox was called in to help Dr Huey who was the family GP. I think my parents either intended to go or did go to Marienbad in Czechoslovakia when I was taken ill and they of course rallied round immediately.

I was in bed in that room for a long time and above my bed hanging on the wall was a large brass electric battery clock with a pendulum under a glass cover. I suppose I remember it so well because of the hours I gazed at it! Very occasionally it stopped and I felt this was a bad omen – and maybe it coincided with bad news. At any rate I have ever since disliked clocks that have stopped and I always try to get them going immediately. There is no doubt that such events affect one for years or indeed for ever.

In time I recovered sufficiently to go away to convalesce and I was sent to a hotel in Bournemouth where I stayed with my keeper (I do not know whether she was a nurse or not) for many weeks. All this happened when I was five so it is not surprising that I remember little of it.

In 1929 we moved from Lansdowne Road to 35 Wilton Crescent in the heart of Belgravia. It was a corner house and therefore had plenty of light overlooking Wilton Crescent on one side and a small square the other side of the road on the other.

The author's mother.

It was a rather grand house. You entered through a small outer hall and then ran into the main hall floored with white marble from which the dining room was entered on the left and the library/sitting

The author's father.

room on the right. The staircase was straight ahead and was carpeted in red and there was a fine mahogany banister rail supported on cast iron pillars. It was quite a feature as the rooms on the ground floor must have been ten feet high. Less formally the stairs descended to the basement where there was a library/study for my father and the kitchen and related rooms. On the first floor above was the best bedroom for my parents, dressing room, bathroom and a large formal drawing room. On the floor above were nice bedrooms for us and yet further up on the third floor were rooms for the servants.

There were usually five servants, a cook (always called 'Mrs') and her assistant scullery maid, a parlour maid and two housemaids. The parlour maid looked after the dining room and served meals and drinks etc. The housemaids looked after the house, cleaning, bed-making and the linen etc. They also lit and tended the open coal fires in the principal rooms which was important as there was no central heating or other form of heating, save for gas fires, which I think we had in the nursery on the second floor. The cleaning and fires were completed before the household got up, so the housemaids were about from 5.30 to 6.00 a.m.

The cook was the senior among the servants, unless there was a butler, which happened from time to time. The cook originally was usually Irish and cooked abominably. Vegetables were always over-cooked and boiled served awash with water and meat too was always overcooked. It was often boiled (and none the worse for that), for instance mutton served with onion sauce or silverside of beef. My older sister Joyce's pet abomination was 'squares of meat' being a form of overcooked beef stew. Potatoes were usually served boiled and often had 'eyes' left in them. Suet puddings were frequently served in the form of spotted dick or syrup pudding (delicious!) or just long grey sausages of suet (disgusting!). Milk puddings with rice or junket were also served. There is no doubt that diet was influenced by the lack of heating in the house and suet keeps one warm. One always wore woollen underclothes and frequently thick woolly sweaters.

Breakfast was a good meal. We often had eggs (without bacon) sometimes with wonderful kosher beef sausages from Selfridges, bright red in colour (and still available!), kippers and rarely other treats. These dishes were laid in the dining room for us to help ourselves, kept warm on a copper tray with meths burners beneath. Electric hotplates came in much later. Bought-in cooked foods like meat pies, most sausages and other made-up dishes we eat so commonly today were avoided because it was thought they might be unwholesome or actually bad and not infrequently they were!

A greengrocer was normally a shop with vegetables and fruit and shelves onto the street uncovered and unprotected from weather or dirt. Potatoes were always sold straight from the farm with the earth on them and vegetables including salads were sold unwashed and usually had many beasts in them. Nor was there any system of grading for size or quality and they were not wrapped.

My mother dealt with the housekeeping in consultation with the cook, frequently ordering food by telephone from grocers (rather good ones in Sloane Street selling coffee and other things) and from greengrocers and from the butcher (who was called De'ath). She would also order from Harrods. It was thought that ordering by phone was risky in that you did not get the best cuts of meat etc, and that it was better to go and do that sort of shopping personally. All this was the subject of daily meetings between my mother and the cook first thing in the morning to sort out the menu and the requirements.

Early on most meals were served in the nursery and had to be brought up by the maids. For breakfast in those early days we often had porridge and rarely cereal, though I remember at some time a cereal called 'Force' was introduced. We were never allowed to eat bacon, pork or ham as my mother was brought up in a fairly strict Kosher way. However she was tolerant of other things like mixing meat and milk. We never had shellfish. In fact I never had bacon, ham or pork until I went into the Army and just did without at school when these were served.

The scullery maid was usually very young (children left school at thirteen) and inexperienced and was concerned mostly with washing up and cleaning. She was essentially the 'scivvy'. In view of the state of the vegetables it was mostly left to her to clean them, remove the beasts and get the eyes out of the potatoes. Many root vegetables were used in the frequent stews and these also required a lot of work in preparation. Washing up was a major task in the absence of dishwashers and the chemicals now frequently used to remove grease etc. It all had to be done by hand with soap and elbow grease. I suspect she was also much engaged in dealing with the kitchen range which was fired by coal and was very temperamental. Cook was not best pleased if the oven temperature had dropped in the middle of baking her cake!

Likewise cleaning the house was laborious as there were no vacuum cleaners. At some point hand-operated brushing machines were introduced, but these took a lot of effort to use and they were no good for the staircase, which had to be brushed by hand.

Foxie (Miss Foxhill) came some time in the early thirties and was a great joy to us all including my mother and it was she who looked after us – and continued to do so for many years. She became a member of the family. She had a great sense of humour and I remember years later, when there seemed to be a great noise in the roof, her saying 'Those are spiders stamping around in the attic!' In the late 1930s she married Kenneth Gwyther who was an engineer building the London Tube railway and he sometimes took me down to see the tunnelling going on.

The burden of looking after us lay largely on her as we saw little of our parents. My father was a successful solicitor in partnership in the City with Herbert Oppenheimer and Arthur Vandyk and in 1929 entered Parliament representing Bethnal Green as a Liberal. Of course prior to that he had worked hard in the constituency and in the political world to establish himself.

He kept a mare called Madeline in London at Smith's stables just behind what was then St George's Hospital (and is now the Lanesborough Hotel) close to our house. She would be brought to the house at around 7.00 a.m. by the groom Connor and he would ride in Rotten Row. When the House of Commons was sitting he sometimes rode to Westminster to reserve a seat for the coming day. Generally a member cannot reserve a seat and nobody has a right to a particular seat (except by custom very senior Members such as ex-Prime Ministers), but by ancient custom at that time you could reserve a seat on the day of a sitting by placing your hat (top hat I think) on a seat in the early hours of that day. So this is what he did! My father was a great believer in tradition.

Joyce and I also rode in Rotten Row when in London from the same stable, which was large and flourishing. The trouble was that

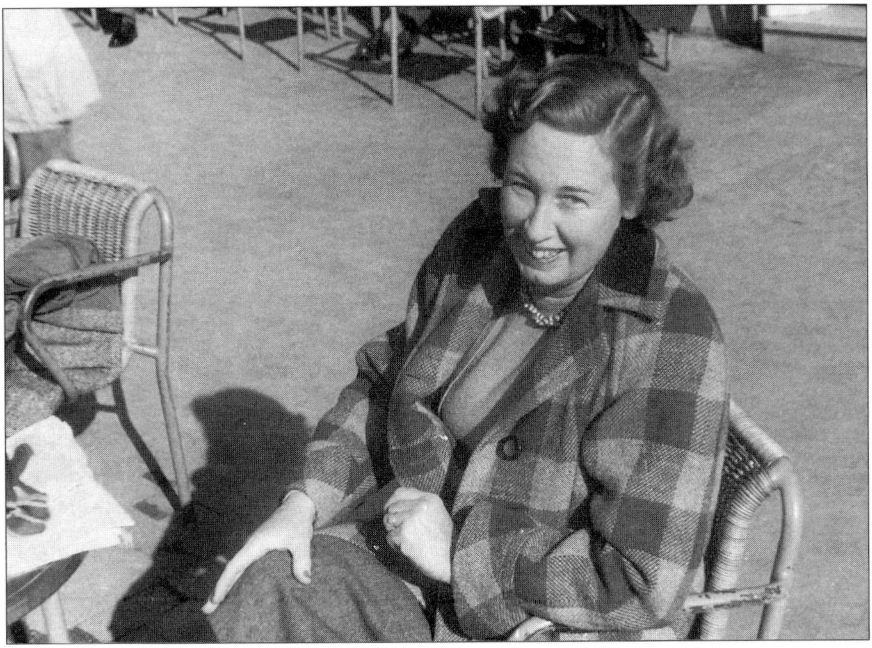

Foxie.

the ponies hired to us knew exactly where one had to turn particularly at Hyde Park Corner and as a result they did and I did not! I frequently fell off there.

My mother became a Member of the London County Council for Bethnal Green as a Liberal at the same time as my father became an MP, so she was rather busy too. Her father, Carl Stettauer, had been a Member of the LCC as a Liberal so this was very much in the family tradition. Carl Stettauer, whom I never knew, was also active in the Jewish community. When the Russian pogroms took place early in the century resulting in the emigration of so many Jews to this country and elsewhere, the Board of Deputies of British Jews, then and now the representative body within Anglo-Jewry, asked him to go to Russia and report on the situation which he did and the reports are still kept, I believe, in one of the libraries.

My mother's family some time back had come from Germany and she had many relations there, which is why we all became so intimately involved when Hitler arrived. One of her relations became a prima donna in the Berlin Opera – Josephine Polly. Some of her music books came to me and I recently gave them to Arabella Nathan in view of her operatic career. Arabella is a daughter of my cousin Peter, son of Cyril, my father's brother. She studied at the Guildhall School of Music.

My parents bought Old Kiln at Churt in 1923 as a country cottage. I regarded Churt as my real home and loved it. Indeed immediately after the war, when I was in the Army abroad, I received a letter saying they were selling Churt I wrote in the strongest terms registering my disapproval! They were impelled to do so because they decided to give up Wilton Crescent which, though not destroyed by bombing during the war, was in a bad state and Churt was not big enough to accommodate the furniture they had, my father's library which was quite extensive or his London prints which he had collected over his lifetime. Indeed his library of London books and prints was the largest and most important in private hands. Nor was Churt large enough or suitable for the extensive entertaining which they intended to do as they had in the past. Perhaps also in the aftermath of the war it was accepted that the successful lived in the country and had a farm. Rotherfield fulfilled all these requirements and was indeed a splendid house.

Churt was a particular joy because it was small and intimate. We had coal fires in our bedrooms lit in extreme weather conditions and in case of illness. Much of the furniture was of oak and antique and much of it is now here at Collyers – including the grandfather clock and the hall furniture.

Old Kiln had an interesting history for our family. Originally two or three cottages, it was converted by Philippa's architect great-uncle Delissa Joseph (who also built the Central Underground Line Stations in London) into a house, which in due course was owned by Robert Solomon and Ethel, my wife Philippa's uncle and aunt, from whom my parents bought it. We stayed there for some twenty-five years and it was then sold to a family called Rose, also related to Philippa, who eventually sold it. So one way or another it was in the family for nearly a century! I have a piece of pottery which came from the Kiln which was just behind Glaisher's cottage.

It was a long house to which a high and lovely full height hall

Old Kiln, Churt.

was added by my parents. There was a large beamed sitting room and a small dining room, which would seat eight at a crush. And there was a nursery at the end.

A terrace ran the length of the house bordered by formal flowerbeds and at the nursery end a circular bed with a sundial in the middle, which is now at Collyers. Beyond that was an arbour covered in roses in summer. Beyond the terrace the ground fell away to form a rockery and there were narrow paths leading to small ponds filled with frogspawn at the right season and streams between were crossed by arched rural wooden bridges. Beyond that there used to be a field. But around 1935 my father decided to have major work done (I think by garden contractors Toynbees) who introduced a stream with small waterfalls from the distance falling towards the house and bordered by two very large flower borders and wide paths of grass. On the border by Sandy Lane rhododendrons were planted which made a wonderful show.

The Head Gardener had always been Glaisher who had been a

Sergeant Major in the Army and was a man for whom we all had respect both as a practical and hardworking gardener and as a man who lived in the cottage at the entrance to Old Kiln. I cannot remember what assistance he had before the major reorganisation, but afterwards I remember we had five men working in the garden. This of course included not only the area of which I have written, but also the vegetable garden which lay behind Glaisher's cottage and over the road where there was an extensive vegetable garden and where the chickens were kept. There was also the tennis court and surrounding area including a long path with cordon apples and the front circular drive with a lawn and rose beds in the middle. These were ordinary, but decorative roses designated by Herbert Oppenheimer with disgust as 'cabbages', he being for so many years President of the Rose Society!

It was from here that in the early years every summer we were taken to the beach hut in Littlehampton by car on most days. My father had a series of fawn Austin 20s which had a glass division and in the back two jump seats. I think baggage was put into a fixed trunk on the back. There was no boot as we know it today. The Chauffeur Pursey who was with my father for many years drove it and it was a rare privilege to sit in the front with him.

My mother was a keen driver having started on a little Singer before the first War in 1912. She never drove the Austin, but had her own car, often a Rover from the early 30s, but in about 1938 she acquired a Talbot with a semi-automatic gearbox which cruised comfortably at 60 m.p.h. We went on holiday to Ireland in it that year.

But to return to our expeditions to Littlehampton. The car – or at least the earlier ones – had a thermometer on the top of the radiator at the front so you could see it as you went along. Bury Hill was a real test for the car which likely as not would boil over and we would then have to stop for it to cool down. Going past Fisher Street on the way I remember there were chickens crossing the road and it was there I learnt the answer to the riddle 'Why did the chicken cross the road?' – 'Because she wanted to get to the other side!'

Lucy used to accompany us on these expeditions often enough. Lucy was about my mother's age and was a great friend. She was the sister of Robert Bernays who was one of my father's (Liberal) closest friends. Lucy married in the mid-thirties Ashley Brereton who had a business in Brazil at San Paulo, so later she went to live there. She taught me to cook on a primus at the hut at Littlehampton and in particular scrambled eggs. She taught me the remarkable fact that if you stir clockwise the eggs scramble, but if you then stir anti-clockwise they do not unscramble! She was a really good cook and made chocolates with cream inside to a professional standard. She was a great personality and had she decided to have a public career would have gone far.

It was in 1933 that my mother and she decided to go on an expedition to South America – just the two of them. They went by Blue Star Liner to Buenos Aires and then by train to the Iguazu Falls in Paraguay and thence through the interior of Brazil to Rio and home. I suppose they were away for six weeks or so. It was in those days a great adventure for two unaccompanied women to venture to the interior of South America. It was while they were away that my father broke out and bought a Frigidaire for Churt, one of the very early refrigerators. I remember the excitement well! My father, though not a gimmick guru, liked to be up with the times.

During the school holidays we hunted frequently with the Chiddingfold Hunt of which Richard Barlow became Master in the early thirties. I suppose I started hunting – on the leading rein no doubt – when I was about seven when we rode ponies from the stable at Beacon Hill with the owner Mr Kirby. I never liked him much. He had a very clear idea that one got the best view of hunting by standing on a hill and hoping hounds would come in that direction. For him it had the dual advantage that it was less exhausting than following hounds and that it saved his ponies from too much exercise and therefore feeding! Later we went hunting following hounds and I thoroughly enjoyed it and often enough my father came too; he was very keen and although not an expert horseman was enthusiastic, courageous and vigorous on a horse.

Harold Capel who was the groom at Beacon Hill Stables started at some point to take us out and he was a great companion as well as an excellent horseman, teacher and carer of children so that added to the enjoyment. Hunting moved up a gear when I was twelve and

I had Chatham who was a magnificent-looking chestnut, strong and beautifully made, but not thoroughbred, five years old, fast and bold with a wonderful temperament. He was bought for me by my Uncle Cyril and really was the ideal horse, we learnt much about hunting together. At the beginning I remember he had the unfortunate habit of 'dropping a shoulder', which was guaranteed to put me on the ground. Together we learnt to jump, to open gates and we schooled each other. Harold loved riding him and of course there were long periods when I was at school and not riding so he enjoyed himself and schooled him well. During the war he stayed at Honeymead which is my sister's country home in Exmoor and served as shepherd's pony with great success as he was so easy to teach and opened gates perfectly. After the war he came to Rotherfield, but by then I was rather too large for him. But when a friend from the Regiment (Richard Le Sueur) and I rode from Tunbridge Wells to Shaftesbury where he lived in 1949, he rode Chatham and I rode a large and most uncomfortable Percheron appropriately called Vanner. At that time petrol rationing was still in force and the roads were pretty clear. However we were mostly off them going to Wisborough Green and then over the Downs to Buriton where we found a purple-faced man in a drive hammering at a deck chair. It turned out to be Archie Bonham-Carter at Buriton Manor who introduced his elegant wife as 'a Zulu' (I gather she had come from South Africa) and was very welcoming though we were trespassers. He found us grazing for the horses and arranged for us to stay for the night in his hotel in Petersfield. I believe that years later when confronted with a rating review he claimed the reduction on the grounds the Manor was haunted – and won! We crossed the New Forest and then went along the Wiltshire Downs to our destination. I took the horses back by milk train travelling in the box with them. Water and hay were available and brought to us at halts on the way as a matter of routine. It was then that I learnt that milk from Kent went to London and from Somerset to Kent!

I was brought up with dogs; first there was an Airedale and then there was Jean, a tiny smooth-haired terrier who travelled with us to and from London. I was very fond of her. I do not know why my father took it into his head to have a number of dogs at Churt kept

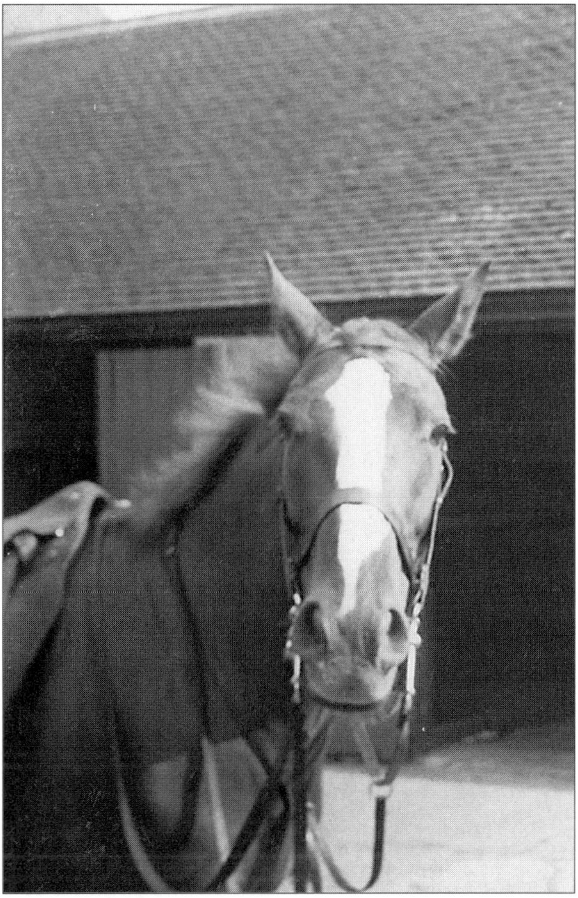

Chatham.

in an outside kennel with run; they were rarely allowed into the house as my mother was not keen. At one time we had an English Setter called Biff, a Boxer called Boxer, a Black Spaniel called Punch and a Great Dane called Tiger. During the quite short times I was at home from school or elsewhere I was expected to groom them all before breakfast!

It must have been shortly before or after the war started that my father had in mind selling Churt. I well remember a distinguished diplomat coming to discuss matters with my father. Tiger and I sat quietly in the background and then Tiger behind my father's chair did everything quietly and without fuss. Shortly afterwards our guest wrinkled his nose and enquired whether the house was damp, to which my father, fully aware of events, replied with the memorable non-sequitur: 'No, it is freehold!'

When we were at Wilton Crescent I was, at the age of seven, sent to a particularly disagreeable day school where there was much bullying. One thing I learnt there was to open the lid of a desk and have my head put into it and then someone would sit on it and bounce up and down. Why no one was seriously hurt I cannot imagine. Luckily when I was eight in 1931 I was sent to Pinewood as a boarder. Among the boys there in the lowest form with me was Harold Sebag Montefiore whom I could not stand. I am ashamed to say that I put his head in a desk and sat on it. I believe I am one of the few people then and later in life he treated with respect!

It was while we stayed at Wilton Crescent that we were involved in activities which I greatly disliked. For instance we had to go to children's parties where one knew nobody and often enough play 'progressive games'. Round the room a number of games were laid out and one had to go from one to another. I cannot remember what they were, but I do know I was thoroughly bored by them. I remember that in the drawing room at Wilton Crescent such a party was laid on by my parents which I found pretty awful. I think I probably found the other children pretty awful too! On one occasion we were taken to a party given by the Ellis Franklins and on being collected at the end, our hostess Mrs Franklin saw me off at the front door and said in the kindest way she hoped I had enjoyed myself and that I would come again. My response was immediate: 'I do hope not!' It was some twenty years later that Mrs Franklin told me this story when I went to play quartets at her house after the war.

In 1931 I went to Pinewood School. There were some remarkable people there. Nurse, Matron and Roy Wakeham were the pillars of Pinewood. It was at Farnborough opposite the aerodrome, then used by the RAF and about 12 miles from Churt where we lived for much of the time. Between them these three remarkable people had a more profound influence on my life than almost any others.

Nurse was a vast woman of, I suppose, around thirty who enveloped one in her capacious arms and bosom where one was entirely safe. To be scrubbed by Nurse was an experience not to be forgotten. We were usually two to a bath on first arrival and she would come scrubbing brush in hand and when she had done we were not only clean, but felt clean – with a reddish tinge to the skin.

She was the kindest person one could wish to meet and if one was in trouble it was to her one went for comfort and support. You did not lie twice to her, she could tell a mile off. It was not that she chastised anyone, she never did. But her disapproval was so devastating it just was not worth it. Indeed it was the force of her personality which instilled into us at the beginning that there was right and there was wrong and the difference between the two. I do not believe she had what would now be called a proper education and I suspect that she left school as most did in those days at thirteen, imbued as if by magic with a sense of morality and a respect for knowledge which some pursued with great success and others not.

Nurse presided not only over the bathroom and the dormitories, but also over the gas ring on the same floor where there was an annual ritual of making marmalade for the year. A huge cauldron of boiling Seville oranges and sugar was stirred endlessly by us all under her supervision. February must have been the time for this ceremony and even now I can conjure the scent, which filled the school at that time. The orange skin was quite finely cut by hand and then the pith and juice poured into the cauldron to make the delicious product which we enjoyed for the rest of the year.

This was just one means by which we were forged into a family. And they were happy times.

There were six or eight boys in a dormitory of which there was a captain. One made many friends among them. Some brave souls from time to time would get up in the night and through the window climb over the roof of a glasshouse or conservatory and take a tour of the garden in the middle of the night, but I never heard of any harm coming to any one as a result. Generally we were a fairly law-abiding lot.

Every dormitory was adorned with pictures – reproductions of the world's great artists – whose names we had to learn. I remember Titian's Bacchus and Ariadne and Pisanello and Rembrandt and Constable and the Hay Wain and Gainsborough and Reynolds. Every term there was a test you had to pass about them and this provided a lifelong knowledge – albeit superficial – of these great works.

Nurse was never addressed by name, but always by 'Nurse'. Her name in fact was Amy Johnson which caused us all a good deal of mirth as there was at that time a world-famous woman aviator of that name, who was rather slight of build and flew, I seem to remember, solo to Australia in a Tiger Moth – which Nurse could not have climbed into, nor would the plane have taken off!

Matron was quite a different sort of person. She was, I suppose, around forty and I imagine quite well educated. Her name was Mrs Mucklestone, a widow who was much respected and liked by the boys, but more remote from them than Nurse. I imagine her main responsibility was in organising the dormitories and everything connected with them and the staff, and in an emergency perhaps the housekeeping generally, although there was a housekeeper whom I remember from time to time.

One such was a Mrs Dunne whom I disliked and who kept telling us how tasty the food was and to eat it up. One day pudding was suet with dates which was horrible and she was coming round telling us all how good it was and taking a spoonful to show how delicious it was. Seeing this, I prepared her spoonful by adding copious quantities of pepper and tendered this to her saying the pudding was horrible. She took a spoonful and ate it and then turned purple with rage – and pepper! I never had any trouble with her again.

Matron had a black spaniel, which as she was reversing her car one day, she ran over and killed. She was naturally very upset. So were we all and the whole school joined with her in her sorrow. This was just an example of the close community which we were.

Roy Wakeham was also, I suppose, in his thirties; a large man with red hair and a florid complexion who had false teeth on a plate which came adrift from time to time as he was teaching, to our intense delight!

I have no idea as to his education. He was a brilliant teacher. Immediately he entered the room to take a class it lit up with expectancy. It did not matter whether he was taking French, History or Maths or teaching the piano, he had the art of stimulating enthusiasm and interest. To us it seemed he had an immense range and depth of knowledge; above all he was able to communicate it and engage our interest. He was an enthusiastic, if rather inaccurate, pianist. I used to have piano lessons and I think the teacher was a Miss Dalrymple who, as I remember, taught one to play the notes, but failed to inspire one with any great enthusiasm for the music she was teaching or indeed music at all. Roy Wakeham would however sit down at the piano and play (albeit not very well) and one was fired with a passion to express oneself through the music and do it well.

He also had the knack of inspiring small boys to think new thoughts. I remember he made us all in the sixth form give a talk on anything we liked and put me on to a book in the library about future science (or perhaps science fiction!). I remember it dealt with the future of coal and gasification and the particles of matter and the possibility of transferring things – and people! – by dividing them up into particles and then reassembling them the other end. And so this is what I talked about and have remembered ever since. This perhaps is the present answer to our rail problems!

Of the other teachers there was Captain Tuck, conscientious but inspired, who taught us maths. In particular he taught us a really useful lesson by requiring at the end of each sum to put at the bottom left hand corner of the page the magic letters 'LT' which stood for 'looked through'. This meant that we had looked through the sum – not reworked it – to see if the answer was reasonable. If you put down 'LT' and you had not looked it through you were beaten (in theory anyway!). With the introduction of calculators and computers years later this discipline has become ever-more relevant. I found that the highly qualified Chief Accountant in our firm produced figures which were not just inaccurate, but millions out – because he had not looked the result through to see if it was reasonable. I told him he should be beaten!

Each year the school put on a Shakespeare play and I particularly remember *The Merchant of Venice* because I had the part of the Prince of Morocco which I greatly enjoyed. My opening lines (and I write them now by heart)

> 'Mislike me not for my complexion
> The shadowed livery of the burnished sun ...'

had a ring about them which is unforgettable. And then there were the caskets and 'all that glisters is not gold ...'. Not only the part and the language, but the clothes were magnificent, all made in-house by whom I know not – perhaps by Matron and her staff. There was nothing shabby about them. I had a 'silk' turban and silk baggy trousers in really bright colours and all the rest of the cast was equally well attired. It was all great fun and taught one how to speak in public and be heard. We put on three performances having had rehearsals for many weeks. Roy Wakeham again was the mainspring and inspiration for all of this.

But life at Pinewood was not all work and no play. The school had quite extensive grounds and in an odd corner a concrete circuit had been built by the boys which we improved from time to time to simulate Brooklands which was then the motor racing circuit par excellence.

We built out of Meccano chassis of cars with springs, originally semi-elliptic leaf springs, and later coil springs and an extended steering wheel so that you could run the car with the steering wheel on a rod. Whilst there was competition as to who could get round fastest, the real interest was in the design and making. We learnt a lot.

Then there were boats to be sailed on the swimming pool. Some were bought in, but many were made by the boys or parents. Most were motor boats as sailing was not practical. I was lucky that Kenneth who was an engineer, husband of Foxie who looked after us at home, built for me out of sheet zinc a model electric motor boat about three feet long. I never painted it. It had a Stewart Turner motor and wet battery and was really Queen of the Fleet and I kept her for many years. That was one means of teaching oneself soldering and the elements of electricity – connecting up in parallel and series and getting polarity right! It was, however, hard on my mother when she enquired what I would like for my birthday and I replied 'a sheet of zinc'. That would have floored most mothers, but not her; I got it!

The headmaster was Cyril Ranger of whom I saw little and did not much like. He owned the school, I believe, and did some teaching, but was not seen much by us boys. He arranged for us to have a model electric railway on a wooden platform built by the school carpenter – a Mr Boditch – and we had to build the track and the signals etc. This was towards the end of my time and so I was one

The author as Prince of Morocco.

of those in charge and had to do much of the soldering of the connections and assembly of the railway lines. I remember – all too well – on one occasion picking up the soldering iron (one heated it in those days over a flame, not by electricity) by the wrong end and the skin of my hand stuck to the iron. That was an occasion for a rushed visit to Nurse *and* Matron!

Another boy (David Lloyd George, grandson of the great man) and I started up a school paper for which we wrote articles and secured some from inside and outside the school. We typed it and then duplicated it on the Gestetner machine which the school had. It was great fun and we learnt a lot. I noted on seeing a copy recently that among the sub-editors were Duke Hussey (now Lord Hussey, one-time Managing Director of *The Times* and Chairman of the BBC) and Anthony Caro as Arts editor (who became Sir Anthony as a leading sculptor)!

David became a great friend. He suffered eczema severely which was an enormous trial for him. It was a coincidence that we became friends as my father had been a great admirer and supporter of his grandfather who had a house at Churt and we were invited from time to time to his house.

Lord Tenby, the younger son of David Lloyd George (the great man) had David and another son, William.

David died around 1983 and the title Tenby was taken by his brother William, whom I met and saw many years later in the House of Lords where he was prominent in organising the cross-benchers.

But my greatest friend at Pinewood was David Storrs. We were roughly the same age. His father was in the Army in the Education Corps as a Colonel and posted to Singapore so his parents were delighted to allow him to come home with me and spend holidays as part of our family.

We came home from school on Sundays every other week or so. My parents used to drop us off at Frensham a couple of miles from home to walk the rest of the way to get up an appetite and get rid of excess energy. Opposite the house – Old Kiln – we had the woods and some sandy-soiled land where we would often go to dig a trench and burrow, in which we would smoke bracken and eat Walls ices bought off the 'stop me and buy one' tricycles which were then common. A plain ice with or without wafers was two old pence. David used to stay with us for many holidays and we had a lot of fun together. We used to go on long bicycle rides together and we learnt the country pretty well. Smoking bracken in pipes made us feel very adult – and sick!

Years later I stayed with his parents in Bovey Tracey where they

David Storrs.

had a house and I remember washing up with him and having a long and full discussion on transubstantiation and doctrines of the Church. It came very naturally from him. Having met David at Pinewood our paths diverged as he went to Clifton and I to Stowe, but he often came to stay with us and frequently dropped in unannounced, particularly in London, for breakfast! My parents had a great affection for him. We did not see much of each other during the war. He was in the Parachute Regiment and was dropped at Arnheim from which by a miracle he got out and was awarded an MC. After the war he went to the Royal School of Mines and after qualifying got a mining job at Avoca in Ireland where we went to stay taking Jenny, who was a few months old. By this time he had married Heather by whom he had three children – Libby, Sarah and Guy. We had a fine time in Avoca and it was routine that when, as frequently happened, a rat crossed the floor of the kitchen David would get out a .22 rifle and attempt – unsuccessfully – to shoot it. The risk of injury to us from ricochet did not seem to occur to him! The main rail line from the north to Dublin came through Avoca where there was a small station. If friends wanted to get on the express passing through, David would shout down to the stationmaster to stop the train so that they could get on. This too was routine and worked well! David then got a job in British Columbia supervising in one of the mines there. I believe to get down to the working level you had to descend by a circular track inside a sort of cylinder with a Land Rover. One day he did this too fast and was seriously injured and died. This was in the early fifties. This devastating news was given to me immediately by Heather by letter to Camden Hill where we were then living, and I well remember feeling shattered.

It must have been around 1938 that we went to Paris by air. This was by Imperial Airways (the predecessor of British Airways) who had two large biplanes called Hannibal and Hasdrubal; I suppose they took around forty passengers each and flew from Croydon to Le Bourget. One was weighed before getting on board to ensure the plane was trimmed. On board there were tables for four with large wicker chairs and lunch was served by stewards as on board a ship. It was very luxurious and the journey took some two hours so lunch was not hurried.

It may have been on such a trip or some other occasion that we stayed at the Hotel Meurice which was very old-fashioned and luxurious – indeed I believe during German occupation it was taken over by the German High Command. At any rate, we were to go to Sir Robert and Lady Mond's apartment where we arrived around 11 a.m. and were greeted with pink champagne and smoked salmon. I was warned that lunch would have many courses and that I should pace myself by the number of knives and forks laid in my place. I saw four and so tucked into the first course. By the fourth course I found we had only reached the salad, and two more sets of four knives and forks were laid to complete the twelve-course meal.

Sir Robert was a brother of Alfred Mond, the first Lord Melchett of whom it was said that, having been denied high office in Government, he declared that if he could not rule the British Empire he

David Storrs and Heather.

would have to create his own and thus formed Imperial Chemical Industries. It is rather extraordinary that his great-grandson Peter should have been the Director of Greenpeace, opposed to the use of chemicals – or GM crops – in agriculture.

I went to Stowe in 1936 in the bottom form and I remember writing home to say I did not think much of the teaching – a view I maintained throughout my time there. Very early on there the headmaster came to take a lesson as he always did. As he came into the classroom of these first-term thirteen-year-olds he drew from his sleeve a silk handkerchief amply sprayed with scent, reciting the while from Horace – ('dark care riding behind him'). I remember writing home that Sunday telling my parents of this and saying 'this was not my style' – nor was it!

The main school building was a palace and we fed in big rooms with ceilings painted like Rubens; they were magnificent and the grounds had been laid out by Capability Brown with lawns and temples all about – now owned by the National Trust. Music was centred on the Queens Temple which had a marvellous first storey, approached from outside by splendid steps and with a parquet floor. The acoustics were excellent. Practice rooms were below in a sort of vaulted crypt with a hideous echo.

I took School Certificate exams (roughly the same as GCSE or O Levels) in around eight subjects including music, all except one of which I passed without any particular glory except Geography which I failed. Many years later it was therefore a particular satisfaction that I became a Fellow of the Royal Geographical Society of which for a time I was on the Council.

I went on to the sixth form specialising in classics. I was not nearly as good as others at Latin and Greek and took a special interest in Ancient History which is the subject I took for entry to New College. Among others in the form were Anthony Barrowclough and Peter Henderson.

I had first met Anthony in the under-tens cricket when he was at St Edmund's School, Hindhead, and I was in the Pinewood team because there were only ten of us under ten! Later as I say we were in the same form at Stowe and at New College together. He went to the Bar and I had a lot to do with him then, eventually he became the Ombudsman. He was not only a first-class lawyer (he got a First at Oxford), but also brilliant at all sports, getting into all the teams at Stowe. Peter was a quiet scholar whom I greatly liked and in time he also went to the Bar. He then came to the House of Lords as a 'Parliamentary Servant' and in due course became a very good and much-liked Clerk to the Parliaments. He was wounded in the war, having served in the Guards; and on retiring early from Service to the House was, most unusually, made a peer. As such he made support for the disabled his main subject.

He asked me whether his daughter could come to my office to see how solicitors worked as she intended to go to the Bar (which she did and practised, I believe, primarily in immigration law following the family tradition of helping the under-privileged). I told Peter we were absolutely full up and I could not think where we would put her – unless she was slim and under four feet ten. She was! She came.

Every year there was at Stowe a prize for essays in different subjects and the one for Classics had the title 'Were the Romans patriotic?'. The first thing I did was to write to Selfridges Information Department (which they then ran to give advice on any subject) and put the question to them. They however were unable to help! So I set to work and found the first difficulty was to define what was meant by 'patriotic' (it is no easier now!). I completed an essay which I thought very unsatisfactory so I tried the History Essay which was on Puritanism. Although not in the History Sixth I was perfectly entitled to do this and worked very hard to get it done in time. I was therefore amazed – and the History Sixth horrified – that I won it!

I had done a lot of music at Stowe where the Music Director was a remarkable man, Dr Huggins. He was of the old school in that he had money and did his job for enjoyment – and worked very hard. The School Choir consisted of every boy, though we had a Madrigal Society. Every year there was an inter-house competition, all boys singing for their House – usually folk songs or the like. I took charge of my House, Chatham. There was of course the School Orchestra and we had very good subscription concerts when, for instance, Sir Adrian Boult (conductor of the BBC Symphony Orchestra) would come and conduct us and Malcolm Sargent, a leading conductor and an outstanding pianist, gave us a recital. Years previously when at Pinewood my mother had taken me to the Robert Mayer children's concerts given regularly in London by Malcolm Sargent.

At Stowe I did quite a lot of composition (and took O Levels in music) and I started up a series of evening concerts – I suppose four a term – in the Aurelian Room which was an annex to the library and a perfect room for chamber music. The performances were entirely by boys, except for Miss Radice who played the viola with notable lack of skill! She was little older than we and was very keen to help us. I never knew how she came to be in the school being neither a teacher nor an administrator. By an extraordinary coincidence a cousin of hers by the same name became my clerk many years later in the House of Lords, and Miss (Lona) Radice came to see us at Collyers not long ago. I was glad to find she is still full of enthusiasm – and indeed I think for some time flew her own plane!

But to return to the concerts. A number of boys were composing as well as myself and once a term we had a concert consisting solely of home-grown compositions. This must have been unique. Of course there was also the need to arrange music for curious combinations of instruments, as we had to cater for what we had. I remember towards the end of my time there supervising prep in the common room and writing the music for such an arrangement. This gave rise to no comment, but was taken as being entirely normal. I believe in other groups it would have been regarded as eccentric or exhibitionist. Acceptance of this was part of the consequence of Dr Huggins' reign, making music and music-making normal for all.

My mother had encouraged me in my musical interest and acquired in the early 1930s a very upmarket clockwork gramophone in a beautiful walnut case – a very good piece of furniture. She had a considerable collection of 78 rpm records including much J.S. Bach which she really enjoyed. The reproduction must have been appalling, but I enjoyed it greatly. I cannot remember when we acquired an electric gramophone, but even then the reproduction was pretty poor by modern standards. Nevertheless the library of records expanded to include most Beethoven Symphonies and Piano Concertos, the Violin Concerto, the *Messiah* and much else. I knew them so well I could tell in advance with all the records when they would finish and it was necessary to turn over.

I suppose it was in the mid-1930s that I was taken to the Albert Hall to hear the *Messiah* conducted by Beecham. He stood on a box with a brass rail to prevent him falling over backwards! I followed the words in the programme while listening to the music – as I have found best since with most choral works – and was overwhelmed by the whole experience. I have an idea my mother thought I should leave after a certain time as it was too long for a school boy, but I would have none of it and stayed wrapped in it till the very end.

I think it was in 1938 that my mother took me to the Three Choirs Festival at Worcester which went on for about a week. I was enthralled and heard for the first time Elgar's *The Dream of Gerontius* and was bowled over by it. In the evenings we went to the chamber music concerts. I think my mother found it rather exhausting, but I was completely absorbed and found sublime what I heard. It was a great experience which has stayed with me all my life.

Stowe was a curious school – marvellous I found for music as I have said – but not one I fell in love with. I was in Chatham House, separate from the main building and purpose-built, rather institutional in architecture with a number of dormitories for around twenty and a common room with wooden armchairs and large rectangular tables. It was there that I wrote the music arrangements during prep in my last year.

The House Master, Ivor Cross, was an old stick and disciplinarian who was a Liberal in politics and keen on our doing current affairs; he organised the House debates from time to time. One of these was on Abyssinia and Mr Eden's (Foreign Secretary) policy of standing up to Italy – and the Germans. Ivor Cross knew of my father's involvement in all this and his support for the Eden approach so, perhaps purposely, he made me lead the debate for the Chamberlain approach of appeasement. I wrote to my father and asked him to tell me what to say as I had been brought up by him and others on the Eden side of the argument. My father rallied round and wrote a brilliant speech for me on the Chamberlain side!

When my father was made a peer he asked me, as was customary, to the lunch party before his introduction to the House of Lords and to attend the introduction. I went to Ivor Cross to request permission for absence for the day. This was in 1940 and I was seventeen. The news of the peerage was of course prominent in the newspapers. Cross pondered over my request for a long time and eventually came out with the memorable response: 'Yes, you may go this time, but see it does not happen again'!

When I went up to Oxford in 1941 my political activities focused on the Liberal Party and the following year I became a member of the Council of the Party representing the universities.

It was not surprising that I should have joined the Liberal Party, which had a lot of very nice members, because my father had been a member and his father, who had indeed been a member of the National Liberal Club, had presented them with a golf cup which I saw there and may indeed still be there. My father was an admirer of Lloyd George and was close to him after the war and a great supporter. There were many cartoons of them both together; the one I particularly remember is of LG driving a motorcycle combination with hair flying and my father in the sidecar with his considerable bulk perilously overflowing!

My father had many friends who were active in Liberal politics and he invited them to Churt for informal tennis parties on the grass court we had there. This was how I came to play my first game with Dingle Foot, one of the five remarkable sons of the patrician Liberal figure from Cornwall, Isaac Foot. He was a tremendous orator in the old tradition who could rouse an audience to great moments of fervour. Dingle was not a very successful QC, but became active in the Labour party, politically very much in the centre, and I think became Attorney General. I liked him a lot. When we were at Camden Hill his widow came to tea with us, sat bolt upright on the straight-backed chair and was a delightful guest, but very formal! By a curious chance his brother Hugh, who became Lord Caradon after being Governor of Cyprus before the Greeks took over and the split with Turkey, and who was UK representative at the UN, made his maiden speech in the House of Lords on the same day as I. It was, I thought, superb and delivered as his father would have done and it kept me enthralled. Another brother John who became Lord Foot was a quiet and thoughtful man, whom I came to know quite well in the House and greatly liked. Yet another brother Christopher was a solicitor in Plymouth and I used to meet him in London when we were both articled; he never did much in public life having I think rebelled against the family tradition. I never met Michael Foot who became Leader of the Labour Party and was not a great success. He was a brilliant writer and literary critic.

Another member of the other Liberal contingent I met at the age of around eight at Churt was Alan Sainsbury. I always liked him enormously. I went to his memorial service at St Margaret's, Westminster and there was a great congregation, Alan having been much-liked in the House of Lords and having died at over ninety. Lord Roll – of a similar age – gave the address and recalled Alan's philosophy in the business which he had built so successfully. The purpose of his business was to provide a service for the community; it was necessary to make a profit and to be efficient to enable the business to carry on. But profit was not the main purpose and object; it was a necessary incident. I found this refreshing and it coincided with my own approach which perhaps I learnt from him and my father in my earliest years.

LG lived at Churt at Bronedee just above the Pride of the Valley Hotel and as children we went there from time to time for tea. We met his second wife Frances there who came to tea with us many years later at Collyers. She was quite elderly and delightful, but rather formal. At that time we had a Labrador who had recently had an operation to his behind and was wearing a lampshade round his neck, charging unseeing into everyone and everything. Frances wrote to thank afterwards for inviting her 'to our gracious home'; we thought this was rather over the top with the dog in a lampshade!

David, who had been such a friend at Pinewood, became ill and died young. William became Lord Tenby, a leading figure with the cross-benchers in the House of Lords and a friend of mine there.

I indeed consulted him about standing for the election of hereditary peers and his advice was to do so. He stood and was elected. I decided eventually, and despite pressure from friends from all parties, not to stand.

A fellow undergraduate called Pollard and I started a Liberal Review at Oxford and we had some rather outstanding contributors. Pollard was of Hungarian extraction and his father was Professor Michael Polanyi of Manchester University, an economist, and it was no doubt through him that we had such contributors as Professor Hayek.

I remember on my appearance at the Council meeting of the Liberal Party, to which I was elected to represent universities, proposing nationalisation of the railways on the grounds that they were a public service hopelessly under-funded by the private companies which owned them, resulting in their derelict condition – that a unified railway system was necessary and Government should provide the funding. This of course happened after the war. I also proposed the nationalisation of the steel industry on much the same grounds which again happened after the war.

After this meeting of the Council a kind senior member asked whether I would like to join the Reform Club, one of the major clubs in London. It was a great honour which of course I accepted and no doubt my father paid the subscription. At nineteen I must have been far the youngest member. Of course I did not go there until after the war, when I went from time to time. It was, I thought, supposed to be a rather radical membership as distinct from the Tory connections of the Carlton. After the war I went to an election party there and was horrified that a Labour win or (worse still) gain was greeted by loud boos and Liberal wins (which were pretty rare) likewise!

Women were not admitted to the club except on Friday evenings for dinner and then kept behind a screen so that they would not pollute the main part of the dining room. I took Philippa there on such an occasion shortly after our marriage to show off this great institution of which I was a member. She was so angry at the way she was put behind a screen that I had to resign from the club if I was to remain married!

Looking back now it is rather extraordinary that in 1941 when the war was not going well for us, and we stood alone with Europe overrun by the Germans, that there was a movement for a 'federal Europe' to come into effect after the war. It was of course implicit that the UK would take the lead. Exactly what 'federation' meant was not clear or indeed discussed, but it was essentially a political concept for uniting into one unit the numerous states which had been overrun by the Germans. It never occurred to anyone – and certainly not to me – that we would not win the war.

It was rather natural that I should be interested in this as my father had taken the lead in galvanising overseas governments in exile here to back the war effort – and in particular those of Poland and Czechoslovakia. Indeed I had a unique experience at our home in Wilton Crescent of having dinner with Mr Benes and Jan Mazaryk (the President and Foreign Secretary of Czechoslovakia). The President was a reserved and quiet man whilst Mazaryk was jolly and outgoing. He 'fell' from a window many years later in Prague when the Communists were in power, and was killed. My father arranged lunches at the Dorchester to stimulate his efforts and secure support from the leading figures in the UK; the organisation was called the National Defence Public Interest Committee. This was the context of his elevation to the House of Lords.

Every night on the BBC the National Anthems of all the governments in exile were played (as well as our own, of course) and it was a formidable list. The contribution to the war effort made by them was great. For instance I met one of the Divisions of the Polish

Army at the foot of Monte Casino in Italy, which they stormed and captured successfully though with many casualties. The Czechs made a great contribution in the air and when recently we were in Prague, I saw in the cathedral a memorial to those who had fought with the free Czech Air Force.

The horrors of the Nazis were well known to us even though knowledge of the gas chambers came later. My mother's family had originally come from Germany and many relatives were there. At Churt in 1938 I remember two girls around ten years old came to live with us having escaped from Germany. The mother of one of them also escaped and brought with her a pair of Zeiss field glasses which she gave to me. I had them round my neck throughout the campaigns and consciously took pleasure in finding enemy targets with them!

The impact of the Nazis on Jewish refugees was also brought home to me because in my father's office he had established under one of the Partners, who was Jewish and who spoke German – Eric Wolff – an office to facilitate the reception and 'processing' of the refugees which acted closely with the Home Office (the responsible department). Very large numbers of refugees passed through this office and I met many of them years later. One was Hans Kornbery who became (improbable as it may sound) Master of Christ's College, Cambridge after considerable opposition. He proved to be a devoted Master to the students and the College. I met him first when, after I had completed a report for the RSA on Energy and the Environment in 1979, he invited me to lunch and to join the Royal Commission on Environmental Pollution, of which he was Chairman and where I remained a member for ten years.

The Anglo-Jewish community mobilised itself to assist the refugees through the Central British Fund for Jewish Relief and Rehabilitation in 1933 when the German Jewish problem started. It gave great practical help to refugees as well as providing to the Government financial guarantees to ensure they were not a burden on the British taxpayer. They also carried out vetting and processing procedures as my father's office later did. The cream of the Anglo-Jewish community was actively involved; it was started by the Schiff family, Alan Montefiore and Oscar Joseph as prime movers and the secretary was from the beginning a young girl, Joan Stiebel, who is still living as I write and devoted her whole working life to the CBF. I became treasurer of it in around 1959 and subsequently Chairman. By the time I became involved most of the Jewish refugee work was completed or hived off to a special committee running old age homes and the like. The majority of the work in my time related to new problems and particularly to the movement of Jews from Arab countries where they were persecuted or in difficulty, to Israel. I spent four days without sleep in Morocco with other members and Joan Stiebel touring Casablanca, Fez Meknes, Marakesh and other cities with Jewish populations to assess the situation. At one small place we found the rabbi in this Sephardic community had trained at the Gateshead Yeshiva! All this was of course long after my Oxford days.

However, the background of the Jewish problems of the 1930s and the early years of the war made a deep impression on me and provided an underlying motivation for me in the war years and campaigns. And then of course the Holocaust became known as fact and that only compounded Jewish consciousness and concern. These were the underlying reasons which led to me to accept an invitation to become a Warden at Berkeley Street (one of the most important synagogues and leaders of the Bafornum Movement) in the years following the war, to the astonishment of the family! As I was living at Churt and riding and hunting a good deal it meant frequently giving up Saturdays, and therefore hunting, to go to the synagogue.

I was at that time an Articled Clerk aged twenty-five and therefore far younger than the usual middle-aged warden. Technically the duties of wardens were to carry out ceremonial at the services in the synagogue and to have responsibility for administration. Ceremonial included carrying the scrolls around the synagogue. It was the custom in Orthodox synagogues to bow to the scroll as it passed, but not in our Reform procedure. On one occasion Alan Montefiore, a senior and much-respected member, was carrying a scroll immediately behind me and a number of congregants were bowing to us, which Alan abhorred; and in a stage whisper echoing round, he said 'Are you God or am I?' Rabbi Reinhart was the senior rabbi who one day was reading the Torah from the scroll at the reading desk when he was constantly and unexpectedly interrupted by the choir, hidden as usual by the screen behind him, saying 'Amen'. I was standing by him as was my duty and I suddenly realised that I was swaying back and forth pressing each time the signal button to the choir. One day in my office in the City I received an urgent phone call from the synagogue asking me to come quickly as Reinhart was having a fight with the (female) receptionist. By the time I had arrived they had fortunately been separated. There was a lot of ill-feeling in the synagogue about Reinhart and at the end of my term a great meeting was held and he was expelled – and started a new synagogue in Westminster. This was not the sort of atmosphere which I appreciated.

I had hoped and thought that intimate activity in Jewish religious life might have given me an experience of the sublimity I had experienced in listening to music, but it did not. And after my term of office expired I played little part in synagogue affairs.

In the early part of the war those of us who went up to Oxford prior to call-up were offered a course for a War Degree. This enabled one to stay for four terms and take a series of 'sections', that is, single exams, one for each term in any mixture of subjects chosen. I started with history with a tutor called Wyckham Legge who was a dull old stick and I did Napoleonic wars with him for the first term. I went to lectures on the naval war with a lecturer called Atkins who started early in the morning when he was usually drunk and brilliant! He was one of the best and most gripping lecturers I have ever heard. One time he lectured in the afternoon and was sober (very unusual) and dull!

I heard that David Ogg had a great reputation as a scholar and specialist in the English Civil War so I went to him for a term, but I found him rather heavy going. David Cecil was tutor in English and had a great reputation for scholarship and eccentricity, so I went to him for English and that was really interesting and stimulating. In preparation for my last term and exam he gave me *Paradise Lost* and I worked hard on it with great enjoyment, partly at Exford where we stayed in the cottage attached to the Crown Hotel right on the Green. I well remember reading the thundering verse of this great work, being interrupted by a furious voice emanating from and through the glass of the telephone box on the green some yards away. There was a furious row going on over the phone and it was Sir

Robert Waley-Cohen in full flood! Sir Robert had bought Honeymead in the middle of Exmoor shortly after the first War as his country home, with a large old farmhouse and several thousand acres of moorland which he improved into grassland for grazing sheep. His techniques were for years regarded as models of how this should be done. His son Bernard inherited the property. Joyce married Bernard in 1943. Bernard became Lord Mayor of London in the early sixties and was made a baronet. On his death a few years ago their son Stephen inherited the title.

When I returned to Oxford after the vacation David Cecil greeted me with a face a mile long to say that to his horror he had learnt that there was no exam in *Paradise Lost* at the end of this, my last term. He advised me immediately to get advice from the Warden. The Warden was a very nice man, but known for his lack of decisiveness; his lodgings were known as 'the sign of the other hand' for this reason. However, being told of my trouble he was instantly decisive and clear in his advice. 'With only four weeks to go until the exams there is only one subject to take, and that is Politics.' So I did under an excellent tutor, who was I think a German refugee called Falk. He was brilliant and I worked pretty hard and passed. This true story stood me in good stead when I became active in the House of Lords many years later!

At the same time as studying these various subjects I took music (theory and composition) under Dr Andrews, the college organist, though there was no exam or 'section' available for this. I went to seminars by the Professor Sir Hugh Allan who was killed in a car accident later in the war.

When I went up originally I took my upright piano which my father had given me three or four years earlier, and I had it in my first room at 6 New College Lane. Although I played the piano quite a lot, my main interest for a long time had been the violin. Early in my time at Stowe, my violin teacher Loris Blofeld had said I should have a better violin than I had and recommended to my father we go to a retired Naval Commander in Kensington for a violin. This we did and went to an upper floor room where there were glass cases full of violins. We bought a JB Vuillaume made in the early 1830s. I think it cost my father £75 which was then quite a lot of

Joyce.

money. It is a superb instrument and Loris Blofeld used to borrow it when he was broadcasting as it was better than his own! Such an instrument becomes part of one and I could not sell it even though I would now get around £30,000 for it!

After a term or two I moved into college to the ground floor at 8 Old Buildings – on the staircase of what is now the Senior Common Room. I was playing a Beethoven piano sonata (I remember it was Op.90) when the door opened and in came the professor, who said, 'That is not how it goes' and sat down and played the whole for me. I was – and am – deeply impressed by this because he was so committed to his very junior students.

I had learnt the violin with Loris Blofeld at Stowe and continued with him as he lived not far from Oxford near Radley. With him I studied for the professional exams at the Royal College of Music. In the four terms I was at Oxford I had not reached the end of the course – and this was no surprise – so I did not take the exam, but it was an experience worth having.

Kitty and Leonard Stein (Leonard was a cousin of my father and a close friend) had a house near Newbury. Kitty played the violin and was in a quartet to which she has recruited an additional viola player to make up a quintet, with whom she asked me to play sometimes. On one occasion there was a summer school for musicians at a school called Down House to which she invited me. A well-known professional string quartet (The Menges) were giving instruction and one of them came to instruct Kitty's quartet. At the last moment her leading violinist dropped out and I was asked to substitute. The work in question was the Mozart Quintet in G Minor as I well remember, so I was landed with sight-reading this. I had played it before, but I found it a challenge – in such company! Somehow I survived as did the other members of the quintet!

Life at Oxford in 1941-42 was as normal as it could be and I took part for the college in rowing, having taken up sculling in the early mornings which I greatly enjoyed. Rowing in a four or eight is a nightmare as you have to keep going however tired, otherwise the boat would overturn and in a race it is worst of all. I well remember feeling as ill as I ever have after the end of one of the races.

There was also the OTC (Officers Training Corps) which was in a sense a continuation of what we did at School. But of course we were taking it more seriously now, knowing that we would shortly be called up, and the training was more rigorous. It was at this time that one could make a decision if one was going into the Army as to whether to opt for Armour or Infantry. I decided on Armour – tanks – partly because the thought of all that walking in the Infantry appalled me! It may seem strange now, but it was assumed at all levels that we would be officers and not first go into the ranks. I have no idea how things are now.

The OTC at Stowe was not a very rigorous exercise though in 1940 it became very active. The Battle of Britain was then taking place and the Local Defence Volunteer Force (LDV) was formed. Throughout the country civilians went out in daytime and at night armed with pitchforks or other available armour to bash the Germans as they arrived by parachute – or by sea on the coast. There was a real belief that invasion was imminent and this was the response. So we went out at night at Stowe and roamed the fields looking for Krauts. That is when I learnt that the cough of a sheep at night is remarkably like that of a human! Most nights we were out for many hours and it was a lovely summer so it was no hardship to do so. We saw the Spitfires in the air going to fend off the attacking Luftwaffe, but never a dogfight. It was all an experience not to be forgotten.

CHAPTER TWO

The Army

I WAS CALLED UP in 1942 and sent to Blackdown Camp near Chobham. Since then I have thought of Blackdown as a Gulag after the Russian style – perhaps unfairly. There was a huge black tarmac square for drill and barrack buildings for dormitories etc. It was a pre-OCTU (Officer Cadet Training Unit) to lick one into shape as soldiers. Therefore there was a lot of drill and some fierce Sergeant Majors. There were about twenty to a dormitory with iron bedsteads and coarse grey army blankets and each morning an inspection when one had stand smartly to attention by one's bed while the bed and one's worldly possessions, which were in haversacks beside it, were inspected as well as oneself.

We were a varied lot in the dormitory – some experienced soldiers sent for promotion and some raw recruits like myself. At that time it was assumed that those who had been on an Officer Training Unit at public school and university were destined to become Officers without service in the ranks. I was determined that I should not be regarded as a soft university entry and therefore when volunteers were called for various sports I opted for boxing, of which I knew nothing. From this fate I was saved by an experienced and friendly soldier who might have been a Quartermaster's assistant who told me not to be an idiot as the toughest and most brutal soldiers were the boxers and I would be slaughtered. I took his advice! There was a good atmosphere in the dormitory and we all got on reasonably well. The great social centre was the NAAFI canteen where they served marvellous hot chocolate.

There was a lot of drill which I quite enjoyed, especially taking charge of drill squads and getting the timing of commands exactly right. One of the Officers there was a Major Dickie Northern who wore green trousers as part of the uniform of his Regiment. I am sure he joined them in order to wear these trousers! He would inspect us on parade and I well remember his turning over the brass buckles we wore on our webbing belts and declaring, 'If you don't polish the backs of your brasses you will die a horrible death'. I suppose he was in his mid-thirties and had never left England. There was another very young Officer – a Lieutenant I think – who declared with all seriousness, 'Napoleon said "time spent in reconnaissance is rarely wasted", but I say, "time spent in reconnaissance is never wasted".' He had certainly never left England!

We were taught to ride motorbikes and to drive. I thoroughly enjoyed the motorbikes riding across country up and down steep hills on the Common and (if I remember rightly) having to lift the exhaust valve when descending particularly steeply. We drove pickup trucks (rather like small cars), fifteen-hundredweight trucks and three-ton lorries as well as armoured cars. I think it was here that while driving I saw another armoured car go off the road on the off side, through a hedge down a slope and come to rest in some trees by a stream. This was John Heath, an old friend from Oxford (Merton), who later went into the Foreign Office and was our Ambassador in Chile during the Falklands War.

I suppose we were at Blackdown around eight weeks before going on to The Royal Military Academy at Sandhurst.

It must have been while I was at Oxford or Blackdown that I was interviewed by Colonel Hurrell of the 17th/21st Lancers about joining the Regiment and I was accepted. The Regiment was equipped mostly with tanks and training was therefore related to armoured warfare rather than Infantry, Gunnery etc. Sandhurst was devoted to this.

Strangely I remember little of life there. Certainly there was extensive drill in front of the great building with its columned portico and range of steps. Regimental Sergeant Major Brand was the quintessential Sergeant Major whose voice was such that, as it is said, when he called us to attention, parades in Aldershot many miles away would do likewise on his command. The ground sloped away from the great building and we were often paraded below commanded by this tremendous voice.

At the end of the parade the Adjutant who was mounted on a

white charger would ride up the steps of the portico entrance and disappear from view there. I gather he and the horse had to practise this for many hours.

We were taught tank driving and the mechanics of the machines. The favourites were Valentines which were very inadequately armed with two-pounder guns, diesel-engined and very reliable. They were however completely outdated.

We had Crusaders which were rather sophisticated mechanically, had petrol engines and big wheels for the tracks whilst the Valentines had bogies rather like a train. The brakes on the Crusaders operated by compressed air. Whilst we did a lot of driving across the country we also used the roads and particularly one long hill at Hartley Wintney down which we came and where from time to time the compressed air system failed, to the alarm of the crew and everyone else. Fortunately I never came across either of these tanks in action.

We were given extensive instruction in gunnery both at Sandhurst and on ranges in Wales. Generally ammunition was stowed on the floor and around the turret and the breach of the gun projected into the turret so that when fired the recoil filled the turret. The wireless operator dealt with the ammunition and loading while the gunner would aim and keep the gun on target (at least in theory) when the tank was moving. During our test firing I must have done something untoward as the instructor nearly lost his hand in the breach. In fact he suffered no injury, but he failed me on gunnery – no doubt rightly. It was therefore with special satisfaction that years later I was appointed Gunnery Officer of the Regiment and there was some discussion as to my becoming an instructor at Sandhurst – in Gunnery!

Map-reading was a course we took and I well remember being taken by the instructor to the place where the test was to be given to us. He pointed out the various landmarks we were likely to be told to identify. The great day came and there was a thick fog so none of the landmarks was visible. Sure enough the examiners asked us where they were and we pointed with total confidence to the directions we had been shown. We passed!

After passing out of Sandhurst as a one-pip Officer (the lowest form of human life) I remember going to get myself equipped with uniform, including Sam Browne, from the Regimental Tailor in Savile

The author on first commissioning out of Sandhurst to 17th/21st Lancers.

Row and being given by my father a handmade pair of brown best calf shoes from Bartleys, where he had his own shoes and hunting boots made. They must have cost the earth, but never fitted properly. On arrival in Algiers about to undergo a twenty-one mile march to our first camp I wore them with great pride, and terrible consequences and great pain for my feet. I kept them for a long time as a matter of pride, but rarely wore them again.

We embarked at Liverpool on (I think) the *Carinthia*, a large liner with many of us on board. Although crowded it was not intolerable. To pass the time sailing to Algiers some of us were asked to, or suggested, talking about things that interested us and I chose epicyclic gears which intrigued me. These gears are used in automatic gearboxes and I think in the steering mechanisms of the Crusader Tank. The audience – a mixed bunch of bored soldiers – took it all very well!

Eventually I arrived at the Regiment which was encamped in an olive grove under canvas at Robertsville near Philippeville. There were around six of us to a tent and we had camp beds and sufficient space for our limited possessions. For washing I had a sort of canvas bucket slung on a wooden folding stand. Reveille on the trumpet awoke us in the morning. The loos (which became an important feature) were a long bench with many holes for occupants, open to the sky. Many of us, certainly shortly after I arrived, had some form of dysentery and during early morning drill parades had to rush to the loos in great distress. Malaria was of course a constant risk and many went down with it despite taking Mepacrine tablets. At some point I had a mild attack. However the main medical problem was the appalling scabby sores which erupted particularly on one's arms. This was a form of scurvy and in time we were directed to take forty (yes forty!) pills a day to prevent this. These sores were quite painful.

Joining the Regiment at this time was not easy as it had recently been fighting a tough campaign which had, of course, welded together those who had taken part, and newcomers were unintentionally regarded as outsiders. To some extent this situation continued until the campaign in Italy a year later.

The Officers' Mess was in a large tent lit by car bulbs powered by a small petrol generator. Dinners were pretty formal affairs and one sat at the bottom of the table with the Commanding Officer in the centre. During our time here the Regiment remained together which later became a rare occurrence.

There were some remarkable Officers who had been in the North African campaign, some of whom I got to know much better later. Commanding was Dick Hamilton Russell who had just been awarded a DSO, a quiet man of great quality who commanded throughout the period in North Africa and for some of the time in Italy including Cassino. He was awarded a bar to his DSO. We all had enormous confidence in him, not least for being unflappable and always sound in judgement. And there was George Ponsonby who was a Squadron Leader and one of the really great professional soldiers I met.

I was in A Squadron and took over the 3rd Troop from John Francis. I had a Troop Sergeant called Himbury who was much older than I, and a regular who had served for many years in India. He was a pretty rugged individual but much respected by all and a wonderful support as I found particularly at Cassino. I remained commanding 3rd Troop until well into the Italian campaign when I was appointed Intelligence Officer. The Troop consisted of around twenty members and had three or four tanks. Each tank was manned by a driver, a gunner, a wireless operator and a commander and sometimes, at least in theory, a co-driver. They were a mixed lot. My driver was a man called Ridge who drove with great force and never let me down, but never changed his socks! There was a mature young man who had been an apprentice printer and quite well educated, and there was Wilde who in civilian life was a farmer, had wonderful eyesight and as a countryman had a marvellous capacity for seeing things, particularly movement. There was a man who might have been a school master called Macdonald. One got to know them pretty well as the months passed and I had a great admiration and affection for them.

This was important because as we fought our way north in Italy we were often on our own as a troop laagered overnight and we slept in the open on our bedrolls. We had of course to maintain a guard all night which we generally divided into four-hour stretches; I usually took the dawn watch not least because that hour is often the most dangerous. I used to cook everyone breakfast of eggs and bacon or whatever was available and served it to them in bed. As a result I was let off other duties of this kind throughout the day!

What could happen – and did on one occasion – was that we were going up a hill across a field expecting to find the enemy when we reached the top. For some reason the track of the tank came off (due perhaps to too tight a turn) which rendered it completely out of action, so one of the troop had to go near the top of the hill on foot and keep guard while the rest of us struggled to get the track back on – not a particularly easy task. The man I sent to be the guard was young and became scared stiff and returned to us shaking. I had to send someone else to do the job. Fortunately we were not attacked while disabled and we got the track on and drove forward. I remember this particularly because everyone rallied round with skill and a good deal of muscle power to do the job. In the Regiment there was a special unit of REME whose job it was to deal with mechanical problems and rescue tanks in the situation such as ours. Of course getting them out – even if it were possible – took time and might itself lead to problems. Everyone in the Troop knew this and motivation to do the job was high!

On arrival in Italy we were encamped north of Naples and were able to witness the eruption of Vesuvius which was not so far away.

We went on endless exercises for a formal frontal attack in conjunction with Infantry over wet ground which became all too familiar to us. Eventually we went in convoy towards Cassino and the Liri Valley. Our convoy was led by an experienced Officer called Rollo Hawkins who unfortunately lost his way. We got onto a narrow mountain track without the slightest idea where we were and had to turn our tanks to go back, eventually arriving at our destination in the valley. There we stayed overnight and I went to chat with the Poles at the foot of Monte Cassino which they were to storm – a really formidable task which they did successfully. There had already been two or three attempts to take the mountain and the Abbey at its peak without success and with casualties. This was to be a major assault.

Dick Hamilton Russell, calm and collected as ever, wanted some reconnaissance done and sent me off in a scout car to explore the terrain. While doing this very close to enemy lines the scout car engine failed and all efforts I made to revive it were unsuccessful. Then there came along an Indian from the 4th Indian Division from whom I sought assistance. I cannot say what he did except cast a spell over the car which then worked, to my great relief!

Bridges had been put in place over the river Liri and we crossed it. After that we went along a track and I was particularly unlucky in going over a landmine although others had passed without trouble. My tank was thus totally disabled and we got out in quick time, fortunately without casualties. Perhaps foolishly I walked up the track to tell my Squadron Leader what had happened and was fortunate not to set off any other mines. There was a lot of gunfire about and the Commander of another Troop of our Squadron, Kevin Rooney, had been knocked out so I was to take over his tank and Troop, which I did. It was not long before my (new) tank had a direct hit, probably from an eighty-eight gun of one of the German Panzer Tank Divisions and we all got out very quickly. Not long afterwards the ammunition went up and that was the end of the tank. I have always been thankful that our tanks had diesel engines as we avoided the carnage which would have resulted from a quick petrol explosion. Two tanks in a single day was not a very good record!

It left me suffering from shock and it was Sergeant Himbury who came to my rescue with words of comfort. The only injury I suffered was a minor one.

The slow fight north through Italy had its moments of fun and sadness. In that summer we often exchanged cigarettes for boxes of peaches and eggs. Cigarettes came up as part of the rations and it was only years later that there were campaigns against smoking and the risk of cancer, so many of us became heavy smokers. On one occasion, I cannot remember why, we remained parked in an onion field for three days cut off from rations and supplies. We ate fried, boiled and raw onions and I rather enjoyed them! You can keep going a long time on onions!

But there were tragic incidents too. We were once parked for the night in a field close to houses and a garden with a fruit cage. One of our Troopers, whom I had known since North Africa, wishing to relieve himself, decided out of modesty to go to the shelter of the fruit cage. As he entered he was blown up by an anti-personnel mine.

On another occasion we were parked temporarily in the daytime with a lot of flak about in some sort of artillery duel. A piece of shrapnel went straight though the chest of my wireless operator. It was a terrible sight and he was still living and breathing with his lungs heaving visibly and losing much blood. I took him in my arms to the field hospital nearby where they mercifully put him to sleep. There was no possibility of survival with such injury. Such experiences never get forgotten and are part of War rarely mentioned in the books.

Dick Hamilton Russell left us and was succeeded, amongst others, by Sir John Marlin. I was Intelligence Officer when he arrived and had to travel in his tank. As IO one had, among other things, to look at air photos and identify problem terrain and blown bridges and to tell the CO. When travelling in his tank one also acted as his wireless operator.

We came to a bridge on a road which had been blown and of which we had been unaware (probably it had just been done), and he required that I pass this information in code to HQ and our tanks. Whilst we received elementary training in code we never used it and it took me hours to translate it into code; I am pretty satisfied that those who received the message never discovered what it was about! Plain speaking and quick reaction was what was required and generally achieved.

But then Val ffrench Blake arrived to take command, a man of great intellectual achievement and great physical fitness who was also an outstanding leader. He was a real joy to work with though he could be exhausting. For instance, we were somewhere South of Arezzo at the foot of a mountain called Monte Lignano which he decided to climb on foot to see what lay beyond. The mountain was a steep grassy slope which he climbed without noticing it, while I struggled up behind him arriving about half an hour later.

In the winter we were in the Florence area and some of our forces were high up in the Appennine Mountains, as Observation Posts. The Regiment was not directly involved. The supplies were taken up narrow rocky tracks by mule and I went up a couple of times. The tracks were stony and often wound round precipices. I do not believe the mules were individually led, but followed in line. I never saw one slip or stop or be in any way difficult, contrary to their reputation. It was a great experience.

Eventually in the spring the time came for the assault on the Po Valley via Forli. We did quite a lot of training in anticipation as the terrain was so different from what we had been used to. In particular the country was flat, divided by canals and rivers. There were great embankments along the waterways to protect from flooding. We practised getting over these embankments in our tanks which was fun but precarious. I still had my excellent driver Ridge (of the socks!) and he would get into bottom gear and use maximum revs to get up the virtually perpendicular incline, then throttle back to teeter on the top and come slowly down the river side where there was usually a reasonably wide road or towpath onto which he had to turn without losing a track on the tank. He was an expert.

Eventually, with Val ffrench Blake in the lead, the entire Regiment raced several miles up a road at maximum speed with guns firing alternately on each side until we were well behind enemy lines and parked in a wood on a hill. It was the most exhilarating experience I had! Where we came to a halt there were a lot of very frightened, very young German soldiers who were no doubt later taken prisoner.

Shortly after this we made our way to a place called Poggio Renatico where I found myself opposite haystacks which I suspected of being camouflage for enemy tanks. In fact I do not believe that they were. At any rate, from some source a shot was fired at us and I was hit in the hand – fortunately only a flesh wound. In accordance with practice (it was before penicillin was readily available, if at all), I sprinkled on sulphanilamide powder and went in my tank back to the MO. There I was helped from the tank (you normally jumped down the four feet or so) and got to the field hospital where there were a lot of soldiers lying on the floor awaiting treatment. My turn came and I was given an anaesthetic (pethidine?) and sown up. It was not long before I recovered and rejoined the Regiment at Ferrara. It was there that on 8 May 1945 we had the news of the German surrender. I was of course delighted when I saw my name among those who had been 'mentioned in despatches'.

Years later (in the 1960s or 1970s) I was paying a London taxi driver when the sharp-eyed man noticed the scar on my hand and asked how it happened. I replied, 'Krauts'! He shook my hand, smiled and drove off. One does not forget such things.

Very shortly afterwards I was ordered to go with half a squadron and all speed to Villach in Austria and to get there before the Jugoslavs, who were, I was told, making their way by train. My job was said to be to save the population from rape. In fact I believe the purpose was to have a presence there and prevent the Jugoslavs or the Russians from including it in their area of influence.

We got up there in quick time and I took over a school for our HQ. I went to meet the German Corps Commander early on who was a fat and flabby man of perhaps fifty. We saluted each other in the accustomed manner and I made it clear he must obey my instructions on which there was no dispute. I never saw Jugoslavs there, but there seemed to be some youngsters getting up to mischief and I was concerned about looting and trouble. I somehow found a woman who might have been a local Councillor and we conversed in French. We agreed that anyone found causing trouble would be put in the local jail and would not be set free except on my say-so. If necessary, I said, I would get my soldiers to deal with troublemakers, but I would much prefer that she and her colleagues see to all this, which they did.

The German Corps consisted of two German Divisions and a Cossack Division – those who now-famously fought with the Germans and returned to Russia to be killed as they did so by the Russians. The Cossacks were on a hill outside the town and in the evening sang as the Welsh might have done; it was a marvellous sound. Very shortly after we arrived I was in our school HQ after dark one evening when someone came to tell me that the Cossacks were refusing to obey the orders of the German Corps Commander and would I go to tell them they must do so. I took a couple of scout cars and two or three Troopers and arranged for two interpreters – one English to German and another German to the Cossacks' language. I arrived at the Cossack camp and was met by, I suppose, the Divisional Commander. I made it clear that they must obey the German Corps Commander and after this was accepted I retired to my HQ. It was one of my most extraordinary experiences, never to be forgotten. Looking back it was rather extraordinary that at the age of twenty-two I should take command of a German Corps and deal with the Cossacks in the middle of the night. It was after this and the accident to which I will refer in a moment that the British Army – and Government – decided the Cossacks should at the insistence of the Russians be returned to them. I had nothing to do with this, but read of it in the press with everyone else. It has always seemed to me that the British decision was right and unavoidable as the Cossacks had traitorously fought with the enemy against their own country and it was quite impossible for the British to deny to their ally the right to punish their own people. I thought of our position if (which was obviously unthinkable) the Highland Division had fought with the Germans and the Russians had refused to hand them to us after defeat of the Germans. Count Tolstoy and others mounted a great campaign against Lord Aldington (formerly Toby Low) who was a staff Officer at the time of the repatriation and he sued for libel and won enormous damages. Aldington was however hounded through much of his life by Tolstoy. I came to know him in the House of Lords years later and indeed we had desks in the same room, and he became rather a friend for whom I had great admiration.

It was after these events that I was going along a mountain road near Villach when horse-drawn vehicles belonging to the Cossacks came in the opposite direction. The driver of the scout car in which I was travelling went too close to the edge of the road which gave way and we rolled over and over, down about a hundred feet. I was knocked unconscious as was he, broke a leg and ribs and woke up in a German hospital in a room with the driver. The Germans treated us perfectly well and in due course decided to set my broken leg (tib and fib). They did not use an anaesthetic so it was extremely painful. I am sure this was not a 'hostile move' and learnt that the Germans did not use anaesthetics nearly as much as we did. In time I was taken to hospital in Rome which was next to the Baths of Caracalla where even at that time superb opera was put on most nights. So I lay there listening – for free – to marvellous performances.

The atmosphere in the ward was excellent and we all got on very well together. There was one patient who had a broken leg and was under traction and a fierce lady surgeon arrived to deal with him. His leg was untouched but he lost his appendix!

It must have been during this time that I heard that Gigli (the great operatic tenor of the time) was to perform with his daughter in Massenet's *Manon*. The Opera House would not have him as it was said that he worked with the Fascists, so the opera was put on, I think, at the Argentina Theatre. It was full. As he came on he was booed. His own and his daughter's performances were superb and at the end they had a standing ovation.

Some time after I returned to the Regiment we were sent to Greece where we were encamped at Lamia near the east coast of Volos. It was a wet and rather dreary winter. However we had there the horses that we had captured from the Germans in Italy and there were two horses I remember particularly. There was Boris, an evil-tempered roan of around 15.2 hands and immensely strong and fast if he wanted to be. I taught him to jump, which he did well when so inclined, but was just as likely to go straight through the jump if not. To my astonishment we had a hurdle race which I won on him and I was greatly surprised to learn that the odds were very short on us! After I was demobbed and the Regiment went to Palestine, the Officer who took him over was killed when Boris charged straight into a jump. The great advantage I had in riding Boris was that nobody else would, so I had him to myself.

Then there was Ham Face, a large heavy chestnut creature who was most amiable, but not much fun to ride. At Lamia one of our duties was to supervise the distribution of food supplies given by the US. They were marked 'Gift' which was a pity, as this is the German word for poison! I decided, as I had on previous occasions, that the best method of controlling the crowds of starving elderly people was that we should be mounted. I was riding Ham Face. The crowds milled around us and he must have had a fly on his leg as he raised it and put it down again. Unfortunately a woman's foot was underneath when he did so and she let out a piercing cry which led to much anger in the crowd. Ham Face was quite undisturbed and stood like a rock. Eventually the supplies were distributed and I thought that was the end of it though I realised that the woman whose foot had been caught must have suffered great pain – it has happened to us all. Next day in the Greek press was a headline referring to the cavalry charge against the peaceful civilians. I must thus have executed one of the very last cavalry charges by the British Army!

1945: Lamia, Greece
Bob English, the author, Dick Tamplin.

It must have been around the time we went to Greece that Mike Heathcote rejoined the Regiment to become Leader of A Squadron, of which by then I was second in command as Captain. Mike was a great horseman and that was his passion in life. He declared that he was going to deal with horses and that I and the Squadron Sergeant Major Woodford, who was a fine Regular soldier whom I greatly liked, should run the Squadron. It worked very well!

It was his predecessor as Squadron Leader, Mike Watson, under whom I served for a long time and greatly admired, whom I overheard discussing a young new Officer with the CO. 'He has not got the initiative and drive we require in our Officers', he said. With much emphasis he concluded, 'Colonel, I would not breed from this Officer'. That was the end of his career in the Regiment.

One of the Army's duties was to supervise the Greek elections, though we ourselves were not much involved. The morning after the election, which had gone quite well, the *Union Jack* – the British

Forces Newspaper – came out with the banner headline 'Disaster at the Polls, one dead'. Later the Greek newspapers came out with 'Miracle of the century, only one dead'.

I was detached for a short time to join the Court Martial centre in Athens where we lived in a very nice villa in Kifissia, a suburb rather higher than the city. Of course it gave a wonderful opportunity of seeing the city and its surroundings. Our job was to represent soldiers accused of crimes, the most common of which was the theft of three-ton lorries. There were general instructions to drivers that on leaving the vehicle they must remove and take with them the rotor arm, thus disabling it. Of course they had a spare and produced the removed part with great showmanship to all around. Off went the lorry to the driver's consternation! On one occasion I was completely stumped for a defence for my client, and without consulting him or anyone else pleaded insanity on his behalf! I was rightly severely told off by the Advocate General who was the acting judge who had some experience, I suppose, at the Bar.

I mentioned earlier US relief supplies. Of course these were diverted by some civilians and went to supply the restaurants in the city so that one could have the most wonderful cream cakes there – particularly at Flocca's Restaurant. They had a branch in Salonika to which in time we were sent and the same excellence of cuisine was to be found there – for the same reason – and in addition marvellous scampi (which I had never had before) nurtured, I understood, on the sewage outfall of the city!

I was ordered to lead a half-squadron into (Greek) Macedonia to quell guerrillas who were fighting there. The country is mountainous and very beautiful. I do not believe we achieved much, but we did meet up with some other detachment and I remember laying on a rather good banquet for them and us beside my tank on an elegant table.

The War being over, the possibility of going as tourists to Turkey arose and the first requirement was currency, so I went to the Bank of Greece to secure some. They said this was impossible as they had none, but kindly suggested I meet a black market dealer in one of the ruins of the city who would fix me up. I duly met him and we did our calculations in chalk on the walls of the ruined building; thus

I got my currency. I went with another one of our Officers – Victor Hill – and we took the train along the coast of Thrace to the Turkish border. There we had quite a party with the Greek border guards and then went on over the border. As we crossed one could see the silhouette of the Turkish soldiers on the embankments, bayonets fixed to their rifles, creating quite a different atmosphere from the one we had just left. The other travellers whom we met must surely have been British spies going back to Turkey!

We found much traffic in Istanbul and a lot of noise of horns blowing. We toured the sites and the Hellespont and dined on fish at the waterside – all of which was a great joy. And we visited the islands in the Sea of Marmora which were then, as now, traffic-free. The magic of dawn there overwhelmed us – as it has when revisiting the city.

In 1946 I was demobbed and returned to England to go back to Oxford to do an Honours Degree in Law, which a grateful country permitted us to do in four terms rather than the usual three years, though the course was the same.

I remained in close touch with the Regiment, which is very much like a family in its personal relationships and a great joy for that reason. I started the London Branch of the Old Comrades and we met several times a year at various pubs and I became a member of various Regimental Committees. The Colonel of the Regiment at this time was General Sir Bertie Fisher who got me involved in the various Regimental Funds – Benevolent, Sporting, etc. This was the context in which, because of my interest in Charity Law and my father's Report on it, it came into my mind that the Regimental Funds might be regarded as charities – one of the categories of charity established by the Act of 1603 being 'the setting out of soldiers'. I pursued this with the Charity Commission and in the result the Funds were established as Charities. This had great tax advantages and gave access to trusts which could only benefit charities. As a result the Regimental Funds prospered.

After thirty years as Treasurer of the Regiment I decided that the time had come to retire. At the annual Old Comrades Dinner, the Colonel of the Regiment (then Field Marshal Sir Richard Hull whom I had known since he was our Brigadier on my arrival in North

Africa) presented me with a pair of silver ashtrays inscribed with the Regimental Motto, the skull and crossbones, which I treasure.

Soon after the war I was ordered (not invited!) by the Commanding Officer to join the Cavalry Club, which I did. We used it a lot for entertaining and it was very well run by a professional secretary. I made no contribution to the administration until our lease was running out and the freehold was about to be purchased to convert the building into a hotel. One day in the bath it occurred to me that if we could get the inside of the building listed this would frustrate the hotel developer and perhaps bring down the value of the freehold to one we could afford. I put this to the Committee and they succeeded in getting the listing, thus reducing the value. We bought the freehold!

CHAPTER THREE

Post War

RETURNING TO NEW COLLEGE in 1946 was a strange experience. It was difficult to realise that there had been so long an interval with such activity since we had left. There were many faces one knew and it was almost like starting again after a long vacation!

Government provided adequate funding and it was decreed that we could take an Honours degree in four terms rather than the usual three years. We were all much older than the usual undergraduates – and pretty mature – and were anxious to get going in civilian life as we were getting old; I was twenty-three and felt it was high time I started serious work.

I was put into 3 Old Buildings in the Old Quad, heated with a coal fireplace and with thick medieval walls. It was a lovely large room which I shared with John Quicke, who became a great friend. He was six foot six, as thin as a beanstalk and was reading agriculture to equip him to run the large family estate in Devon. The winter of 1946 was an exceptionally cold one with a lot of snow. Rationing was still fully in force and there was a severe shortage of coal. We had a hundredweight a week which was just enough to keep the fire going for the weekend. So that is when we lit it, and due to the thick walls, the room remained slightly warm on Monday; thereafter it was bitter and in the evening we sat wrapped in our army sleeping bags which were tied round our necks. I well remember one evening there was a knock on the door and thus wrapped, we both hopped across the room to open the door. There was a thin and nervous maths don who, on seeing these apparitions, fainted quite away and we had to resuscitate him! The loos and washing facilities were in a barn two quads away so we had to go into the open to use them. They were unheated.

Law was a subject new to me and my tutor was Jack Butterworth, only slightly older than I and the rest of his pupils. He became a great friend and after being Bursar of the College, went to start Warwick University which he did with great success and as a result was made a Peer. He was not a great scholar and was to be heard in the basement corridor of the Library declaring in stentorian tones (he never spoke in a whisper), 'There must be something in this philosophy business. I must get round to it one day'. Since the title of our faculty was 'Jurisprudence' we had a good laugh. He was however a good tutor and made us work hard which we wanted to do – there was so little time.

We worked in the College Law Library. It was in fact a very interesting group of most brilliant students. There was Tony Barrowclough; we had been in the same class at school. There was Christopher Slade who to my mind then was an obvious candidate (in the fullness of time) to be a Law Lord.

Wilfred Bourne was the most brilliant intellectually, the type who might have read Greek Tragedy in bed for fun! There were John Balcombe, whom I had known slightly in the Jewish context, and Brian Dillon who I suspect had made his way through hard work and merit with no legal background. Wilfred went into the Civil Service and ended with a Knighthood as head of the Lord Chancellor's Department. Tony had a great career at the Bar where I frequently instructed him on behalf of clients, and ended up as the Ombudsman with a Knighthood. All the others went on the Bench and finished in the Court of Appeal. There was also Willie Pybus, a lifelong friend who had a brilliant academic career winning most of the prizes, who became a Partner with me shortly after qualifying.

When Jack Butterworth became a Peer I organised a party for him at the Cavalry Club (in the double bridle room, not double bridal as I had thought!) with all the above except Wilfred with whom I had rather lost touch. They had all achieved their honours and final positions, so it was a matter of some pride for Jack that he had nurtured such a group. When I told one of my younger Partners about this he asked why I had not invited Robert Goff, who became the most brilliant of the Law Lords, and I had to reply that he was too young by five years; he was after our group as a student of Jack!

Willie Pybus.

It was by chance that some time after I started to practise I was phoned by the Israeli Embassy in August about extradition and a hearing the following day. I rang various Counsel's Chambers without success as then all barristers expected to be away in August. At last phoning Tony Barrowclough's Clerk (whom I knew well) he said he had a bright young man called Goff who had joined Chambers very recently and would I care to speak to him. I did and he said that he knew no more about the bail application which was in point than I, but that if I came to his home that evening in Kensington, by then he would. He did. We eventually had thirty-one bail applications, a hearing in the High Court, the Court of Appeal and the House of Lords, and won all the way. This was his first case!

But to return to Oxford. I resumed playing the violin quite a lot, but felt I never attained the competence I had had previously. However, I had a lot of fun with my own quartet and later took lessons with Marjorie Haywood who was quite well known at the time. I never felt I clicked with her. At any rate this served to enable me long afterwards when Philippa and I were living in Camden Hill to join an amateur quartet organised by André Mangeot (who had a well-known quartet carrying his name and who edited Mozart Quartets). We had a lot of pleasure playing at his home in Kensington Mews and sometimes outside in the roadway; once I remember we played the Schubert Octet in the street!

It was at this time that we invited him to dinner at Camden Hill and Philippa organised duck as the main dish. Quite unexpectedly for us he came armed not only with a violin, but a pianist. It was then that I had to carve the duck so that I had the skin only, to stretch the meat for five!

The food in College was rationed and not very good. To eke out the meat, College served whale meat about once a week. At breakfast time you could smell it cooking and there was a rush to book in at any available restaurant in the town, as it was disgusting. A favourite place of mine was the Taj Mahal in the Turl where you could have a real blow-out of curry – and one did not enquire as to what was hidden behind the hot spices!

The Professor of Law was A. L. Goodhart, essentially a very simple man who wanted to keep in touch with law in real life and sat as a Magistrate. He was a brilliant teacher and of course wrote a great deal. I was asked to review his book on 'English Law and the Moral Law', which I managed without getting into trouble with him. We became friendly and when he was appointed Master of University College some years later I stayed with him. By a curious chance his son Philip, who is a barrister and was made a Peer, served with me many years later on Committees of the House of Lords. He succeeded me as Chairman of the Court of Discipline of Cambridge University.

In the summer of 1947 my father, as Minister of Civil Aviation, went around the world and took me with him as well as my mother. Others in the party were Peter Masefield who had a great deal to do with the creation of Heathrow Airport (which opened around 1946) and later with Gatwick where one of the main buildings is named after him. He was perhaps ten years older than I. Again there was a curious coincidence in that as I was concluding my term of office as Chairman of the Royal Society of Arts, he was active there too, and I was delighted that shortly afterwards he took on the

Chairmanship and was largely responsible for the redecoration and rebuilding of part of the premises. While he was doing this one of the builders forced a piece of furniture off its bracket and was leaving the building with it when Peter saw him and gave chase. It was recovered somewhere near Tower Hill!

We flew in a Lancastrian (a civilian adaptation of the bomber) first to Cairo and on to Karachi and thence the long hop to Singapore. Then we went to Australia, Hong Kong, China and Thailand and back to Karachi and home. It was a memorable trip.

We had many interesting experiences, of which one of the most memorable was that on the way out in Karachi, the British Governor General was there, and on the way back Mr Jinnah, whose photo he allowed me to take. In Australia we went first to Darwin which at that time was very much the 'outback' and consisted of wooden houses on stilts and dirt roads. I found it an exciting place. The place I liked most was Tasmania where there was an Admiral as Governor and I remember that it was there for the first time that I realised my fly buttons were undone as I entered the dining room and retired behind an aspidistra to rectify the situation. As a result I now tend to check when being entertained!

Of course, the idea of a Labour Minister making a visit did not accord with the custom of the Officers of Governors. On one occasion my mother enquired of the ADC whether the Governor expected her to curtsey (this being quite common as he was representative of the Queen) to which the reply was, 'The Governor always expects courtesy from his guests'. He clearly expected wild and unmannerly behaviour!

China was an experience all its own. At the time Chiang Kai-shek had his capital at Nanking and the Communists were making fast inroads into his territory. The British Embassy was in Nanking and one of the staff used to take me riding before breakfast and we saw the (human) dung carts being removed from the city. There is an enormous memorial to Sun Yat-sen in the city where one has to climb enormous numbers of steps to reach the top which we were expected to do. By this time my mother had had to return home from Australia, but my father frequently stopped, as he said, 'to admire the view'. It was a very exhausting climb.

Then came the time when we were to dine with Chiang. I was seated next to him and my father at the other end of the table next to his wife. Chiang spoke only through an interpreter, as I had to, though he understood English well; it gave him time to think. I took an instant and deep dislike to him and believe that he would have knifed anybody without compunction. I would not trust him an inch and told my father so afterwards. As regards his wife, she made me think of her as the embodiment of evil who would poison anyone for the fun of it. I came away with the feeling of relief to be out of reach of both of them! I suppose there are few people now living who met them in the way I did and it was a rare privilege to do so – but not a pleasant one.

I returned home having to face the Finals at the end of my fourth and last term at Oxford so I had to put in some hard work, having spent my long vacation on this exciting trip.

I joined the firm – Herbert Oppenheimer, Nathan & Vandyk – on 1 January 1948, articled to my father. He was not there as he was Minister of Civil Aviation. The premises were at 20 Copthall Avenue to which it had moved shortly after the war, having had to occupy various offices following the destruction of the office in Finsbury Square in 1940. Immediately after their destruction I believe the firm took a suite at the Savoy Hotel, but later found offices in Norfolk House opposite the Law Courts.

I received a very friendly welcome and I already knew many of the members of the firm whom I had met over the years at Churt, or when I went as a boy to the office with my father. Many of the staff had joined at thirteen after leaving school and had worked their way up through the firm. One, Mr Samain for instance, had joined the firm in 1919 and by the time I joined was a senior Manager. Mr Connett had joined in 1912 – the same year as my father joined Oppenheimer as a Partner – and was respected throughout the profession as a leading litigation practitioner. There was Mr Braine, our bookkeeper, who had been there for countless years and who of course kept the books in his own neat hand. When I met him on the stairs sometimes I would ask him whether a client owed us money or not and he always knew in his head, usually with the amount. Computers and accounting machines came in much later.

The Managers were the backbone of the firm. When a boy applied for a job and he was taken on he was told that if he stayed a year and worked hard he would be with us for life. Many were. Indeed, years later in the seventies and eighties I had to arrange a succession of parties to celebrate fifty years with the firm. Victor Hadley was a good example.

In 1932 when there was an economic crisis throughout the world, Victor's father lost his job like so many others – and unemployment benefit was not all it later became. Victor, aged fourteen, had recently won a scholarship and had a bright future at his school. However, faced with the financial crisis in the family he decided to apply for a job which had been advertised by the firm and was seen by Mr Vandyk who was in charge of administration. Mr Vandyk liked the boy and offered him a job in the General Office as a messenger and told him, as usual, that if he stayed a year and worked hard he would have a job for life. Victor accepted. His headmaster came to see Vandyk to satisfy himself that this was a real job and that Victor was not wasting his talents on a dead-end post. He went away satisfied, partly because Vandyk told him of the excellent career so many boys joining the firm had enjoyed. Victor was a great success in the General Office and soon graduated to helping with debt collecting and became an assistant to Mr Samain. He went on training and working under experienced Managers until he became one himself. As he was so good, the firm offered him Articles, he qualified as a solicitor and in due course became a Partner. For his fiftieth anniversary – it must have been in 1982 – I arranged for the Master of the Rolls, Sir John Donaldson (later Lord Donaldson) to come as the guest of honour. Quite a career.

To become a Manager you trained in the profession in the manner I have indicated. There were no exams or qualifications. It was only some years after the war that they came to be called 'Legal Executives' and had to pass exams. Managers were excellent practical lawyers often practising in a specialised field and were much respected within the profession, at the Bar and elsewhere. It now seems remarkable that, leaving school at thirteen, such high educational achievements were possible through training on the job and hard personal effort.

My secretary Margaret Duce (always referred to as 'Miss Duce') who joined me in 1950 just before I qualified and remained with me for thirty-three years until her retirement, was an example of a person very well read, of strict principles, able to play the piano and a very active member of her Baptist Church. Her grammar, spelling and punctuation were meticulous and her typing and shorthand as fast and accurate as any you could find. It had to be remembered that the typewriters were mechanical and the errors led to starting again; there was no possibility of correction as on a word processor. As my secretary she had to deal with clients of every description and had also to deal with a great variety of characters in the firm itself. She left school at thirteen. Sometimes it makes one wonder whether the raising of the school leaving age has been worth it!

A legal secretary had, in addition to these qualities, to know the special forms in which documents had to be produced. For instance, a will was on thick paper with a wide green ribbon threaded through the left top corner and the two ends cut diagonally with sealing wax and the firm's seal placed to secure it on the front. A conveyance had likewise to be on thick paper and laid out in a particular way. Owners of land estates often, even in my day, required that the conveyance to them be handwritten in copperplate on parchment. Indeed my father, when he bought Rotherfield, required this. Firms did not any longer have staff able to engross in copperplate by hand; a special office in the Law Society did this. Pleadings in High Court litigation had to be printed if exceeding a certain length. I well remember I was anxious to delay a case which the other side wished to accelerate and sent a messenger to my office to deliver a pleading. I quickly saw that it was not very long and told the wretched man I could not read it, it was not printed! Instructions to Counsel were typed on Brief paper, which I suppose might now be A3 size, in a special form and enclosures inside it kept in place with red tape. Some documents had to be bound with narrow green tape sewn into the left side which was done with a special needle. A sufficient margin had to be left to enable it to be read. All this a legal secretary was expected to know although the less senior ones often restricted themselves to the requirements of their particular department. Miss Duce knew it all!

It was rare for solicitors, whether they were Partners or not, to have been to university. Neither my father nor his brother Cyril did.

Miss Duce:
the author's secretary, 1950–83.

Articles usually lasted for five years, reduced to three if you had a degree (in any subject). You took your Solicitors Final Examination at the end of Articles. You learnt the Law from your Master and from books during Articles.

Due to the war, Articles were reduced for me to two years. I went round the various departments dealing with property, commercial law, trusts and litigation and it was of course all rather a rush.

One of the unusual things I had to do as an Articled Clerk related to Israel, then recently created from the British Mandated Territory of Palestine. Palestine had been part of the Ottoman Empire for generations and had no modern commercial law. During the Mandate the firm acted for most Palestine institutions and the Mandatory

Government and drafted the commercial laws which were adopted there. During the Mandate many commercial organisations were created mostly by the firm. For instance, Palestine Electric headed by Abraham Ruttenberg, and The Dead Sea Works (chemicals) headed by Novomaisky were constituted as English companies incorporated in England. These had to be transferred to Israel and the task was entrusted to me. Fortunately after some fifty years no questions have been raised as to whether I did it correctly! It was certainly an interesting time.

Herbert Oppenheimer (always called 'HO') founded the firm in 1899 with an office over the Westminster Bank at 1 Finsbury Square. He was a very unusual character. He came here, as so many did in the years at the turn of the century, from Germany. He had been a pupil of Clara Schumann, the widow of the great composer Robert and herself a notable musician and pianist. He told me there had been a question whether he would make his career in music or law. It is remarkable that during the war there were in London at the National Gallery daily lunchtime concerts given by leading musicians including Myra Hess, a top British pianist of the time. At one of these concerts she performed his compositions.

I met her when we were both staying with HO at his house on the river at Bray. He tended to dress formally for dinner and was wearing a dinner jacket. After dinner on this lovely evening he said he would take us out in his punt on the river. Using a punt pole in the traditional manner, he gave us a pleasant evening without getting a drop of water on himself – or us, an extremely difficult thing to do. He was a perfectionist in all he did.

He grew roses at Bray, did the grafting himself and won many prizes at the Royal Horticultural Society shows. He was President of the Rose Society four times, a record I believe.

He was an outstanding lawyer and became very well known in that capacity. Throughout his life he had a very thick German accent and was extremely difficult to understand, particularly when he was, as was usual, smoking an enormous cigar. On his eightieth (or maybe his ninetieth) birthday a young journalist came to interview him and for lack of any other opening to the conversation asked him whether he was not concerned as to the effect of smoking twenty huge cigars a day. 'Yes,' he said, 'I shall die young'!

Herbert Oppenheimer.

His secretary, Miss Whiting, joined him during the first War in 1916 and remained with him virtually throughout his career. How she understood what he was dictating I do not know – nor how she handled his frequent temperamental outbursts, but she did. One evening long after office hours he was seeing a client and there was a great noise coming from his room heard by the Office Manager who was locking up. So alarmed was he that he phoned Mr Vandyk who lived in Kensington to come immediately, which he did. There he found HO and the client in mortal combat throwing books around the room – all because HO was furious that the client would not take his advice! Like most people of genius he was not an easy man, though he was always most kind to me personally.

My parents at this time had Rotherfield and a flat at 55 Park Lane. I spent most of my time at Rotherfield where I worked pretty hard for the Solicitors Final exam particularly. I was at the Law School studying for it. We had horses which when not grazing on the farm at home were kept at Peat's yard in Tunbridge Wells which in its

Philippa, the author's wife.

heyday must have been a hive of activity. I hunted quite a lot with the Eridge and took hunting holidays, transporting a horse to Romney Marsh or elsewhere for the day by box, which I hired. Sometimes I went out three or four days a week riding my father's horse as well as my own on alternate days. It was great fun. Rationing of everything including petrol was still very much in force, so there was not much traffic on the roads.

Then came the Solicitors Final exams which were divided into two sections separated by a week or so. Between these sections I was invited to a great ball at the Honourable Artillery Company (HAC) in the City and Philippa came. We got engaged that night! Philippa's family and mine had known each other for many years partly because Philippa's family firm, J. Saloman, was in the leather trade in Bermondsey and my mother's father Carl Stettauer had also founded a leather firm in Bermondsey. Indeed Philippa and I had met at Churt at the age of five. After the war we met at a party. In 1950 we married. Among her many excellent attributes is an empathy with animals so we always have had horses, ponies, donkeys and dogs as members of the family as well as our three children Jenny Ruth, Nicola and Rupert. To recover from the exhaustion of the exams and the shock of getting engaged I phoned John Quicke and told him I would like to stay with him in Devon for a few days, which I did. It was very restful and I remember, he being a great expert on grasses and having a sick calf, we spent much time plucking the most luscious fescues we could find!

The wedding was on 14 November 1950 and on the same day I became a Partner in the firm. We decided to start life living in London and found a tiny flat in York House near Sloane Square. It was a service flat in that there was a maid and the cost was £35 per month. The oven in the kitchen was so small that when we had guests to dinner one night the chicken would not go in so I had to put my back against its door and shove, thus dislocating the parson's nose! In a few months we found a house at 15 Camden Hill, and the maid from York House and her husband who worked as a footman at Buckingham Palace came to live in our basement. They were wonderful, but when we had a small (or large) cocktail party he would insist on opening the door and receiving the guests in his yellow and black striped waistcoat in the Royal style – which was – and is – far from ours!

One day at a party I found John Walford there (whom I had known all my life) and he said his fiancée needed to live in London in a respectable home because her father was abroad in the Navy. That is how Pegs came to stay with us until the wedding.

The house was pleasant enough, but we found that we always went to Rotherfield or to JB (Philippa's father) at the Poor House in Sutton, south of Petworth, for weekends and holidays to get out of London. It was therefore natural that we should seek a home in the country and thus we found Collyers around five years after going to Camden Hill.

The house and the office were very cold by modern standards and I remember setting the thermostat on one electric radiator we had at Camden Hill at 45 degrees (Fahrenheit!) and that it was almost always on. There were woollen vests and pants called Chilprufe which I always wore in winter. For the office there was a strict regime in the City as to 'uniform'. A dark suit had to be worn with a shirt with a separate starched collar attached by collar studs. I had a number of flannel shirts which I wore at the office due to the cold. A bowler hat was compulsory until around 1952. We never wore 'Anthony Edens'. They went out I believe at the beginning of the war.

After moving to Collyers in 1956 and commuting from Haslemere, one arrived at Waterloo and took the Waterloo to Bank underground which was crowded, but bearable. At Waterloo you had to walk up a very long slope with steps nicknamed 'The Cardiac Ramp' as so many suffered heart attacks on the way up! Escalators were introduced in the mid-fifties.

There was a proper old-fashioned restaurant car on the train in the morning and one could get a full breakfast served by a Pole known as Popski. In time this service was withdrawn, but the coach remained and so four of us who regularly did the journey bought a red tablecloth, coffee and biscuits and enjoyed them daily. When years later I was in Los Angeles talking to the chairman of a bank we were chatting about where we lived and I told him I commuted from Haslemere. 'I know it,' he said, 'and there are four madmen who go every day with a red tablecloth, coffee and biscuits.'

In 1951 shortly after qualifying the firm sent us to Switzerland for me to learn something of Swiss law and German language. HO had extensive connections there and had since 1926 acted for the Swiss Government. He had worked closely with one of the leading Zurich lawyers, Dr Wettstein, and his Partners Dr Berger and Dr Jucker who had their offices in Ramistrasse. My father had given us a Morris Oxford car and in this we took ourselves to Zurich where I remember we arrived during a carnival – the Sechsaleuten! We made our way to the home of Frau Sprecher in Susenbergstrasse on a hill outside the city where we were to stay throughout. It was a lucky choice. Frau Sprecher was a widow who was very strict in requiring us to have lessons with her in German (high German, not *Schwiezerdich*) every day and requiring us to read the leading article daily in the newspaper (the *Neuer Zurcher Zeitung*) which was always difficult and rather philosophical. Her daughter Frau Preiswerk lived there too and her son Titi who was in his teens. Titi had a wreck of a car which was unlicensed and thus could not be parked let alone driven on the road. It was therefore kept in the front garden separated from the road by a hedge. At darkest night we would have to help him lift the car over the hedge on to the road and he would drive around the Dolder Woods with great joy. On his return the car had of course to be lifted back again!

Frau Sprecher was a remarkable person and had recently been President of the Zurich Frauenverein which effectively ruled Zurich. That organisation promoted temperance and its hotels (which were many) were 'dry'. Frau Sprecher had a wide and varied circle of friends. She kept in her attic the music library of Erich Kleiber, the great pre-war conductor of the Berlin Philharmonic Orchestra, and had the Wintertur Quartet to dinner while we were there. She was also a considerable mountaineer, climbing the Matterhorn in her sixties!

Towards the end of our stay she dispatched us to see *Maria Stuart* by Schiller at the Schauspielhaus which was rather like sending an elementary student of English to a Shakespeare play. We could not understand a word and retired to a café after the first act where we stayed until the performance was over and then returned home. We were too alarmed to tell Frau Sprecher what we had done and it was only about three years later when I was visiting Zurich that I did so and we had a good laugh together. Also towards the end of our stay I was invited to call on the senior officer in Zurich of the National Bank and there had a long discussion with him in German on economic and political matters. I really felt then that I had achieved some knowledge of the language which alas I soon lost.

Our car gave us the opportunity of seeing much of Switzerland and indeed participating as onlookers at an assembly in a great open-air arena of the population of the Canton of Glarus where decisions by the Canton were taken in the most democratic forum possible by the entire population in the Volksgemeinder.

The following year I was asked to go to Israel to advise with a barrister, Leonard Caplan. Our host was the Attorney General Chaim Cohn who later became Chief Justice. In 1952 there was a severe shortage of accommodation – and everything else – in Israel. He had great difficulty in finding somewhere for us to stay. Eventually I received a telegram from the Attorney General to say that at last he had been successful and that we had a room at the YWCA (Young Womens Christian Association)! Leonard Caplan and I shared the room. The food at that time was appalling and most meals seemed to consist of heart and lung rissoles varied with gefulterfisch. These troubles were compensated for by the interest of the work, which mostly related to the consequences of the division of Jerusalem between the Arabs and the Israelis with a neutral zone between. What law applied to business operating (or at least established) in the neutral zone which was identified effectively as a buffer between the two main parts divided by barbed wire? Among others there was Barclays Bank! There were questions relating to Exchange Control with which I was very familiar in England and a host of other interesting and unusual questions. I came to have a great regard for Leonard Caplan's knowledge and learnt a lot from him – as well as from the Attorney General whom I greatly liked.

I went to Israel a number of times later with my father and met a lot of interesting people whom he knew well, including President Weizman. It was many years later in 1964, after my father's death the previous year, that the Israel Government invited Philippa and me to come to Israel for a week or more to look around as tourists.

It was a very kind thought. It was on that occasion that I met a Mr Herzog who had responsibility for foreign affairs and who invited me to call upon him for a brief meeting. We got so involved in discussion that the meeting lasted some two hours and was continued the following day. One thing which impressed me was his approval of the ability to receive Arab broadcasts which contained much interesting material; I thought he might want to censor them. The overriding impression given by these visits to Israel was the enthusiasm and idealism which permeated everything they did. It was quite an inspiration and I often think now how things have changed.

We had some exciting experiences on this trip. We were taken towards East Jerusalem and the border with the Arabs and were nearly shot. By contrast we went to the Lebanese border post and I was anxious to see up the coast to the places mentioned in the Bible and ancient history. Our guide took us up the small slope to the Israel guardhouse which was empty and then towards the Lebanese border to my considerable alarm. At the Lebanese guardhouse we found the Israeli guard alone. He said his friend the Lebanese guard was on holiday so he was looking after both sides of the border. What an example to follow!

The City I found a good place to work – rather like a university city. You would go out into the street to get lunch and as likely as not would meet a friend or someone with whom you had connections and have a chat. Those active in the City were fairly few in number and most either knew each other or at least had some connection through a firm. This was the basis of a high degree of confidence which existed between people and business. The phrase was 'my word is my bond' and this was true, but it went further than this. There were few regulations as to conduct and no compliance officers or regulators other than, for instance, in the Bank of England relating to banks and financial institutions. It was rare for there to be a scandal. I used to travel to London on the train quite frequently with a man called Mr Keogh whose job on behalf of the Bank of England was to ensure proper conduct by banks. He knew what was going on by touring the watering holes used by bankers. If he smelt trouble he dealt with it immediately. Mr Keogh was the one man who did this. Thus the cost of running the City was tiny compared with what it became with all the controllers and regulators later introduced by legislation.

As if by some process of osmosis, everyone knew if somebody who was not straight had entered the City and all were on their guard. Indeed it must have been difficult to start in business in the City without some form of introduction. On principle this worried me, but I never heard of a case of injustice or indeed complaint.

My father gave me good advice about the profession. First he said that if you wanted to make money you must go into industry or commerce; there were other compensations for being in the profession, notably the interest of the job and the people whom one met and dealt with. This was true until quite recently when absurd fees started to be charged by solicitors not really doing legal work, but acting as merchant bankers and charging accordingly!

Secondly, he said that by the time I was thirty-five I should be able to deal with anything. By this he did not mean I was to be expert in everything (which would be absurd), but that I should know sufficient in general terms to know the problem and where to seek help. I took his advice and therefore never closely specialised as so many were starting to do. There was one assistant solicitor in the firm who told me his ambition was to be the greatest living expert on Section 4 (1) b of a particular Act. I could imagine nothing more boring.

My interest in Europe and some form of unity there had, as I have said, started during the early part of the war as a response to the war itself and the two recent wars between Germany and France (in 1870 and 1914–18) in the latter of which we had suffered grievously. Therefore I followed the efforts of M Monnet the Frenchman and others after the war to achieve this. In 1954 I went to Paris, called on the British Embassy and saw the Minister there to discuss the then-current talk about the creation of a Free Trade Zone. I explained that I was interested on behalf of our Continental clients particularly in relation to their exports to England, and English clients for export to the Continent. 'My dear fellow,' he said condescendingly, 'this is not reciprocal'! I believe the Foreign Office never had the slightest idea what was going on in Europe and the immense efforts which were being made for years to create the Common Market, notwithstanding the creation much earlier of the Iron and Steel Community.

Hence we did not refuse to join so much as being ignorant of what was happening!

My interest in these matters led me to want, in the interests of the firm, to reinforce our Continental legal connections which through HO were already longstanding. So when we were invited to join the Wisselink Club I accepted with enthusiasm. This club had been started in the early sixties by a Dutch tax lawyer called Wisselink who had gathered into a group one firm of tax lawyers from each of France, Germany, Belgium, Luxembourg and Switzerland. We became the UK members. We met three or four times a year to discuss tax law developments in the EC and our own countries. One learnt a lot. It was useful for many reasons. For instance I remember an occasion when I was asked a question by an American client which we had discussed at a recent meeting of the club, but I could not recall the answer in detail. So I rang the member concerned and told him the situation. Could he remind me of exactly what he had said and as to the answer to the question? He remembered the discussion well and gave me all the advice I wanted. So I rang the American client back that day and he was much impressed! I will refer in a moment to the American developments, but it is convenient to mention here that this was the background against which American clients started to instruct us in relation to matters within the EC, which they left us to handle for them. It was an exciting development.

Of course one became friendly with the members and this was a great joy. For instance the senior French member Delattre (who had a country house in North Brittany) arranged for our children to exchange holidays. Jenny went to him and his son came to us. Jan Kergal who was more junior in the French team had a *manoir* on the River Rance in Brittany and was a keen sailor. I sailed up the Rance to his home piloted by his eight-year-old daughter Beatrix who knew every obstacle and sandbank in the river. The following day he took me in his yacht through the Isles Chausey which belong to the French and are part of the Channel Islands east of Jersey and consist of a large area of rock. There is a way through which he navigated – and subsequently on another trip I did so, to my peril!

In another year Philippa and I went to Brittany by car and visited him. He cooked a magnificent *steak au poivre* on board his yacht – the only time I have succeeded in getting Philippa on board any yacht!

Later they all (Jan, six children and Madame) sailed to Chichester and anchored there from where I brought them to Collyers where we had prepared a great feast in the patio – luckily it was a fine day. They all gave themselves minute helpings and our hearts sank for fear that we would be left with most of the food uneaten. We need not have worried. Being well brought-up according to French custom – rigorously enforced by Madame – the children were taught to take small helpings, but there was no limit on the number! Happily it all went most successfully. It was interesting that they had never had jelly or choc ices which we gave them!

The relationship between all the members was very relaxed. We held meetings in our countries by turn. Once we had them in our boardroom at Copthall Avenue and old Wisselink was in the Chair. He spoke French, German, English and, I think, Italian, appallingly badly. He spoke at some length in English on a tax subject and at the end said to the company at large, 'Don't you think I did that in English very well?'. M Riser, the Swiss member who spoke all these languages extremely well, got up and said, 'Mr Wisselink, you do not speak English, you murder it!' at which everyone laughed and Wisselink the most.

There was no formal relationship between us, but we advised each others' clients as necessary and this worked well. It was a sort of federal relationship with no boss (which suited my temperament far better) and quite different from the formal amalgamations of firms which has taken place more recently.

The experience of the Wisselink Club led me to initiate a similar group relating to EC Law and transactions in which I brought Beno ter Keile from Holland, Nouel from Paris and very good people from Cologne. I formed this years before we entered the EC and it was very effective and educational. When the European Commission attacked the world aluminium industry for anti-competitive conduct one of our clients in the UK was involved. It was largely due to our Common Market Club that we got instructed and when the case was progressing, I brought in Beno when in an English case I would have brought in a barrister. It was one of the major cases before the Commission, which in those days acted both as prosecutor and judge.

The 'prosecutor' in the case was assisted by a very able, but tiresome English lawyer who had a very distinctive and disagreeable voice. Years later I was asked to see whether I could persuade the UK Government to support a Treaty relating to recognition among EC states of charitable bodies. I thought this might come under the Lord Chancellor's Office so rang up my old Oxford friend Wilfred Bourne who had by then become Head of that Office. He said he would put me through to someone who could help. A moment later I heard a voice I recognised immediately – it was my enemy at the Commission! He came to my office and agreed to support what I wanted. So, in the end, he made amends!

In the fifties the Americans were investing heavily in Europe and particularly in the UK. It seemed to me that the many rather large American companies which were setting up here required English legal advice and that we should provide it! I went to New York with my father in 1956 and met many of his friends there including two Jewish law firms. In the US, Jewish law firms – in that all the Partners are Jewish and often many of the staff – are much more common than here. There was a Strook, Strook & Lavan and Proskauer, Goetz & Mendelsohn in particular. Over the years we had a close relationship with both and we acted for many clients introduced by them. Each had the same sort of practice as we and conducted it in much the same way. There was no question for instance of charging contingency fees which was done by ambulance chasers and other claims-orientated practices.

It was on this visit or maybe one shortly after, that Walter Mendelsohn with a leading lawyer from another firm, Beth Webster, proposed me as an Associate Member of the Association of the Bar of the City of New York. This did not entitle me to practise in New York, but to use the Association's facilities there which were substantial and included an excellent library which I came to use quite frequently in later years. It was a considerable honour (as a foreigner) to be invited to be a Member. I am now the longest-serving such Member and some years ago they were kind enough to make me an Honorary Life Member.

In subsequent years I went to the US quite frequently on professional business and I was asked to lecture on international transactions at Stamford Law School outside San Francisco by Dean Spaeth, the head of the faculty. I spent much time in preparation. Stamford Law School is for postgraduates and one of the best. There was tumult when I arrived at the airport. I learnt that the baseball World Series Final was to be played the following day there and that Mays (the Bradman of the game) was to play. I was surprised to find there were any students wishing to hear me, but they were going on to the match later. It was clear to me that they did not want a serious lecture on International Transactions so I asked them what they would like me to talk about. Their unanimous reply was, 'How do you English lawyers charge?' I told them I could do this without any preparation and we had quite a jolly time discussing this and other more interesting subjects! They were a very nice and interesting lot of students and I enjoyed the occasion. I was taken to the match and instructed in baseball and all its intricacies by a judge of the 9th Circuit of the Federal Court of Appeals.

Somehow I also got involved in the Council of Foreign Relations which is a non-official body which arranges lectures on foreign relations subjects throughout the States. I thus had the opportunity of seeing many parts of the country. Two occasions come to mind. First I was asked to go to speak in Seattle. I arrived at the Consul's Office and was astonished to find an old school friend from Stowe who was also to speak that evening. It was a man called Coates whom I remembered was the son of a well-known composer of light music of the time. He was to speak on Turkey which he knew well while I was as usual to talk on the Common Market. I very much wanted to hear his talk which I thought would be much more interesting than mine. So I cut mine short, and my lot all went to hear him!

I had been speaking in Los Angeles and told my friends my next call was in Omaha. They filled me with gloom about this remote Midwestern city where there was no civilisation, only cattle! I flew in and indeed saw enormous herds of cattle. I took a taxi to the city where the main street was so steep the taxi had difficulty getting up it! I expected a very dull and limited audience. It turned out that there were twenty-one universities in the area and it was the HQ of the US Air Force! I had a very large and well informed audience and I greatly enjoyed it. If you live in Los Angeles the rest of the States is clearly regarded as in the backwoods.

I had a very good relationship with Bill Strook. He and his wife had us to their home in Chapaqua, a suburb of New York, when Philippa and I went on our first visit to the USA. We had a close and productive professional relationship over many years. He introduced leading American bra manufacturers who wished to establish manufacture in the UK. I well remember one of our assistant solicitors writing to the clients at length advising on the factors they should take into account and ending with, 'You should also bear in mind the Explosives Act'! When Western Union, the very well-established telegraph company, were ordered by the Federal Communications Commission in USA to divest themselves of their overseas operations I was much involved and had to deal with the disposal of the Transatlantic Cable System (which was I believe the first of its kind) and this involved gaining a minimal knowledge of wireless telegraphy including 'muxing'. It also meant dealing with the numerous landing point facilities in Ireland. It was a big job, and fascinating.

When Bill Strook decided to make arrangements for his firm to have representation in Paris he appointed a remarkable man, Sam Pisar, who had been at their Los Angeles office. Sam originated from Poland and had escaped to acquire postgraduate law degrees in numerous countries. He was a fascinating personality and when in Paris there was trouble between unions and the owners, by some extraordinary chance he was asked and succeeded in resolving the problems. He was also much involved when matters relating to the German concentration camps came up for consideration. Bill made quite firm arrangements with him and we had an informal and loose relationship, so the Strook firm and ours were working on this quite closely together. In the end problems arose and the relationships were terminated. He was certainly an interesting person to know.

Judge Proskauer must have been in his mid-eighties when I first came to know him. He was a leading figure in New York law and in the American Jewish community and was much respected. He was always very kind to me and I arranged his ninetieth birthday party in London with friends of his in the judiciary, in business and charities and the Anglo-Jewish community at a private room in the Institute of Directors, then in Belgrave Square. It was rather a success. On one occasion when I was dining with him alone in his New York apartment he said we were going to the variety theatre in the heart of the city. We arrived at a side door where we were greeted by the doorman who clearly knew him well and he was immediately taken to his habitual seat in the front of the dress circle. The show was put on by the 'Blue Bell Girls' of whom he was a great fan! It was through him that I got a seat in the Carnegie Hall to hear Jacqueline Du Pre, a British world class cellist, play the Schumann Concerto just before she was struck down by MS.

Walter Mendelsohn, Proskauer's Partner and his wife Doli were perhaps ten years younger. From time to time I stayed in their apartment in New York. He came to England sometimes and visited us at Collyers on most occasions. He became a great friend of Philippa and me. He was full of adventure even at his age and he and Doli in their mid-eighties chartered a boat to take them for a couple of weeks on the Canal du Midi which they thoroughly enjoyed.

He introduced a number of interesting and important clients including the American part-owner of the Pan Am Building in the heart of Manhattan, a very prestigious and large new office block. The owner was a Mr Wolfson and he and his wife were delightful quiet people who had me to dinner from time to time. The Chief Executive was Bill Zimmerman whom Philippa and I came to know quite well and to like.

On one visit I was about to make to the USA he asked me to bring hunting gear as we would go hunting in upstate New York. So at vast expense I paid the excess baggage for boots, spurs, heavy coat and bowler hat and arrived thus equipped at the Drake Hotel where I usually stayed. At 4 a.m. on the appointed day I was to be found in the hall of this hotel fully clad ready to hunt. Bill arrived punctually in his vast car and off we went. Bill was wearing a pink hunt coat and at that hour of the morning it was no doubt this that prompted an alert policeman to stop the car and give him a grilling. Eventually we were allowed to proceed and we drove up to a small town in the countryside where we met others who were to join the party. Three of them – a middle-aged Wall Street lawyer (who looked as if he should be playing golf rather than hunting), a doctor and one other got into the back of Bill's car and off we went for another half hour or so into the country. We arrived at the stable yard near to where the Meet (the Opening Meet I think) was to be held. The horses were of a very high standard and Bill had a very elegant thoroughbred. He had, I believe, instructed the stable to scour the Eastern USA for a horse up to my weight and they found a magnificent animal which was a real joy to ride, being beautifully schooled with a mouth as light as silk and very responsive to the slightest application of aids.

The field of about fifty was very friendly and with exquisite courtesy (to my alarm) required that I go in front with the Master. We started off and seemed to go round the point-to-point course in reverse. My steed jumped perfectly. Then we got onto the narrow stony tracks which everyone cantered down without a care for the horse's feet. I would not have gone at more than a walk for fear of bruising, but I followed the customs of my hosts. We came to a post and rails across such a path with a solid shiny rock on the landing side. My faithful steed slowed to hop over the jump and land safely on the rock. He knew it all! Then we came to a field and a hedge in the middle which we jumped without difficulty. But our Wall Street lawyer came off and lay motionless on the ground. Nobody stopped so I thought I should, but fortunately was forestalled by our doctor. He diagnosed that he was not concussed but had become unconscious through fright before taking the jump! I think he broke his arm and the doctor took him back to the car.

We had started about 8 a.m. and finished about 11 a.m.; fifty started and five of us finished! A lot – including Bill – had retired early, but there were a lot of casualties. I got back to the stables and found at the place where the Meet was held steaming cauldrons of stew which all of us ate with relish. Eventually we got into the car for the homeward journey. We had our casualty moaning in the back and the other passenger we had brought up had also apparently suffered a mishap. So three out of five survived in reasonable shape – two having retired early. I gather this was par for the course. I was told that horses only last a very short time here as they quickly become permanently lame from the going. I was horrified.

Some years after this Bill came to Collyers and we took him hunting on Jenny's cob. Having fuelled himself up with one bottle of whisky in his trousers and another in his coat pocket we set off. I think it was somewhere near Bignor Park that I saw him at a perilous angle, liable to fall off and to make the saddle slip round, so I suggested that the horse was very tired and so we slowly made our way home. He said afterwards that he was extremely sore as he was not used to our saddles and I sympathised.

We saw quite a lot of Bill from time to time and we always had fun together. On one occasion when Philippa and I were in New York he invited us to lunch at the Pan Am Building, and there we waited for her to come from the appointment made for her with Revlon, who were to deal with her for free for some reason. The spectre of a doll arrived for lunch, Revlon having told her that she needed 'redesigning'!

Walter Mendelsohn had a younger Partner, Robert Kaufman, who also became rather a close friend. He was elected President of the New York Bar Association and I met him there as I had met other Presidents due to my Associate Membership. They were all leading Attorneys and very agreeable. I would have been happy to have any as a Partner – and most other Attorneys I met in New York. The foul-mouthed creatures seen on television do, alas, exist but are mostly claims lawyers paid by a percentage of recoveries and no doubt some of the criminal lawyers whom I did not meet.

I came across US claims lawyers when acting for a UK insurance company which had become insolvent and had many claims outstanding against it which I was dispatched to try to settle. In doing so I travelled widely in the US. To find the lawyers I often had to go up dark stairs in ancient buildings and find a lawyer who would at first sight strike one as a television criminal! There were many large claims and I remember one for $500,000 which I had not the slightest difficulty in settling for $5,000. There seemed to be no substance in the claim and if taken to court I believe we would have won – and had to pay nothing. But time and cost had to be considered and the lawyer got his thirty per cent of the $5,000 and was happy! Many of the claims were, I thought, manufactured or stimulated by the lawyers rather than their clients. I fear the same is happening here now contingency fees have been introduced; it produces a 'claims culture'.

But to return to Bob Kaufman. Sometime after Presidency of the New York Bar he became an Officer of the American Judicature Association which had a high reputation in the legal world and had many judges and senior lawyers as members. Its prime purpose was to maintain and improve the quality of judges. Generally judges are not appointed as they are in England, but are elected and the electoral process does not always produce the best result. There were therefore questions as to how suitable candidates could be selected for election and similar matters. Discussion went much wider than this at the meetings and these were very interesting. I was invited to be the only non-American lawyer on the Board of Directors and I greatly enjoyed membership.

I remember one discussion on televising court proceedings and everyone was in favour. I felt that pressures on participants and witnesses in having to give evidence broadcast to the world would become intolerable; it was bad enough to have to come to court! Witnesses might therefore be even more reluctant to give evidence than without this. It might dissuade plaintiffs from bringing cases and defendants from defending and thus pervert justice. Juries might be affected by public opinion developed by the television coverage and feel under pressure to give a verdict they otherwise would not. However these thoughts did not prevail!

They were interested in the proceedings of the European Court of Justice as well as our own courts and we had interesting discussions around many such subjects.

The meetings were in various locations in the US and my final appearance with Philippa was in Arizona at Sedona. I received notice about this meeting and how to get to Sedona. One flew to Phoenix and then caught Sedona Airlines to Sedona. Our excellent travel agent in Liphook was very worried that he could not find any record of Sedona Airlines and they were certainly not members of the IATA. Eventually he was able to contact them and booked our ticket. On arrival at Phoenix we enquired where Sedona Airlines were to be found but nobody seemed to know, and we were advised to get on the airport employees' bus as the driver might know. We did and in due course the driver stopped to let us off – laden as we were with a lot of baggage – on the wrong side of a six-lane highway which we had to cross to reach the hut she pointed out. We did and on arrival at the hut found a man in an old leather jacket who announced that he was Sedona Airlines and that their one plane was ready to take us. We took the baggage to the plane and with difficulty got it in and the pilot/owner/boss put us into the two seats available with grave doubt as to whether with the weight of the baggage and myself we could take off. It was very small and had one engine. In time, to our amazement, we arrived at Sedona which is surrounded by red rock and pinnacles.

One of the pleasures of being a member of such groups is that one makes friends – sometimes long-lasting friendships. So it was with this one. Among others the Chief Justice of Washington State was a very interesting and delightful person and we got on well and indeed still exchange Christmas cards. He suggested that we all go in a small plane (similar to the one in which we had arrived) to fly inside the Grand Canyon and get a really good view of this gigantic hole in the ground and the course of the Colorado River. We leapt at the opportunity and had a very interesting and enjoyable time on which I took a lot of photos from the plane. It was only some time afterwards that I learnt that these flights had been stopped because they were so dangerous and there had been so many casualties!

Bob comes to England quite often and to Collyers from time to time. He has a country place in Connecticut where he has a very special vegetable garden with a wide variety of herbs which he cultivates – and fruit too. Every year he sends us a couple of jars of fruit jelly and in thanking him I asked him to praise his wife for her cuisine; I got a reply saying it was nothing to do with his wife – he produced it!

Among his professional connections was a judge who was, I think, Head of the Court Martial Service. He came over with a party and had arranged lunch at the Tower of London where I was invited to join them. That is a lunch venue I had never expected to experience!

Philippa and I went to the US from time to time together, the first time on a holiday provided by my father with the return trip on the Queen Mary – on one of her last voyages. She made the crossing in five days of sheer luxury. One was levered into and out of deck chairs by elegant stewards and we fed in the select small verandah room where you could see others eating their fare in caviar! The food was fabulous and the décor very much 1930s of very high quality. We had a spacious cabin with bathroom. Philippa nearly sank the ship by failing to turn off the bath taps and creating a flood throughout not only the bathroom, but also our cabin. We decided we would have to mop up the worst of it ourselves before seeking help from the numerous stewards!

On that trip we went to Boston and met Jenny Baron, a judge whom my parents knew, who had for that year been elected 'US Woman of the Year' or a similar honour of which she was rightly proud. For lunch we had Maine lobster which neither of us has ever forgotten.

On one occasion we went to Washington to the Supreme Court in session and saw the twelve Justices sitting behind a curved table in black swing chairs, and when they leant back, as they constantly did, they disappeared from view and then came into sight again as they leant forward, like ducks on a pond! Through my father we met Chief Justice Warren for tea there – a delightful and easy man – who had presumably at my father's instigation invited another Justice, Felix Frankfurter, to join us. I knew that he was a difficult and unpopular character and was clearly very prickly. I was told that the Chief Justice and he had never before met except formally and we were therefore instrumental in bringing them together. I doubt that this was a lasting relationship!

It was a long time before I next went to the Supreme Court. That was when I was organising a seminar of the European-America Foundation for about forty people to consider whether the proposition that banking and insurance in the EC should, as the European Commission wanted, be controlled by the EC or by the member states. I knew that these matters were dealt with in the US by the States and not federally and I thought it would be useful to know why and how it worked. Who better to tell us than a Justice of the Supreme Court? So after seeing the British Ambassador who was then Sir Antony Acland (who was later a co-trustee) he lent me the office Rolls in which I arrived at the Supreme Court where, as arranged, I met Justice Sandra Day O'Connor who agreed to come.

Of course, on our visits, Philippa and I went to the sights and museums in Washington and New York and were particularly impressed by the Lincoln Centre which is the heart of music in the city – and the home of the Julliard School of Music. The story goes that a quartet was performing there in the presence of a philanthropist who was anxious to help the School. At the end of the performance he spoke to the members of the quartet praising them and ending by saying, 'Boys, that was a great performance. One day you will grow into a great orchestra'!

We went to the Guggenheim Art Gallery, then a new building for modern art. You started at the top to which you went by lift and then descended a large spiral staircase on the walls of which the exhibits were hung. We found the first was a square of white with one red dot in the left bottom corner. The second had two dots until one reached the great final of three dots. We decided we were too old for this.

We usually stayed at the Drake Hotel which was very central and luxurious where for breakfast in one's room they served Cranshaw melons which were delicious.

However there was an occasion when I went to New York for a charity based in England, at which my chief colleague was Dick Livingston-Booth who was a great figure in the charity world and I believe founded the Charities Aid Foundation. He became a close friend. Arrangements had been made for us to stay at the Waldorf Astoria Hotel which is vast and fairly ancient. On arrival I asked whether Dick had arrived and was told that he had, and his room number. I then asked for my room number and the key. After searching their books at length they said there was no room booked for me and they were absolutely full. Then, helpfully, they said, 'Your friend Livingston-Booth has a double bed; you could use that'. I said he was indeed a friend, but not as close as that!

My interest in Europe and the US led me to join a group initiated by Sir David Nicholson who was an MEP to hold meetings of leaders in Europe and the USA as well as the UK to help avoid conflicts arising between the two particularly as regards agriculture, but also in other fields. It was called the America-European Community Trust. These meetings were limited to lunchtime affairs and were interesting and useful, but I felt could well be extended to weekend seminars for in-depth discussion at a very high level. It was fortunate that Mrs Anne Senior who was active with the Association felt the same way and was very well-connected and knowledgeable.

We formed the America-European Community Association Trust which was registered as a charity. We had a very distinguished list of Patrons – including the American Ambassador – and of Trustees and of members of the Advisory Committee. I was Chairman. Over a few years we held a number of seminars, but here I only refer to two.

The first was held at the Palace of Fontainebleau. It was to this that I invited Justice Sandra Day O'Connor of the Supreme Court of the USA particularly in the context of the growing interest of the Community in bringing banking and insurance into Community responsibility rather than leaving them within the province of member states. In the USA these are generally State rather than Federal matters; Justice O'Connor explained how this came to be and the consequences. We had many other very distinguished participants including the Chief Legal Adviser of the US State Department, the Chief Justice of the European Court of Justice and the UK Advocate General, then Gordon Slynn, who is now a Law Lord and a friend. There were about forty participants and I believe it was a successful meeting. I remember the Legal Adviser saying that he had no idea that progress in community action and the development of the Community had progressed so far and must take this into account. It was this sort of information that I was anxious to promote.

Dinner was held in the Palace. I had no idea that there were no kitchens there or that the arrangements made by the Palace would be so unsatisfactory. The principal guest was the Prime Minister of Belgium who sat on my right and the American Ambassador to France on my left. There were perhaps one hundred and fifty sitting down to dinner in all. After two hours or so the soup appeared. Progress was so slow that I was concerned when we might finish the meal and have the speeches. I suggested to the Prime Minister and the Ambassador that they might wish to take advantage of the facilities whilst we were waiting. This is the first and only time I have suggested to a Prime Minister that he might wish to go to the loo! They were both most grateful.

The other seminar to which I refer is that held in Copenhagen focused on waste and the need to create a satisfactory Community-wide administrative system such as exists in the USA in the Environment Protection Agency. The function was held in Copenhagen with a very high-powered list of participants from the USA, the Commission in Brussels and the UK. We had as Guests of Honour, among others at the dinner which followed, the Prime Minister of Denmark, and the US, Portuguese, French, Greek, German, Irish and British Ambassadors to Denmark, so it was a high-powered affair. Although in due course the European Environment Agency was formed with its HQ in Copenhagen its purpose is rather different from what we had in mind. Who can say what if any effect our seminar had on all this?

After a few years, and when we had held a number of seminars, I retired from it and it wound up. The subsequent development of increasing tensions between the USA and the EC indicate to me that the Association was worthwhile and might have been useful had it continued. Trade disputes which have bedevilled the relationships might thus have been avoided.

CHAPTER FOUR

Legal Practice

WHEN I JOINED HON & V as an Articled Clerk in 1948 the total number of people in the firm was about eighty. Of these three were Partners, namely HO, my father and Vandyk, who were joined by Leslie Cork as a more Junior Partner. Leslie joined the firm from another in around 1933. His family had established an accountancy firm largely interested in the grocery trade and had a substantial insolvency practice. His brother Kenneth succeeded his father as Senior Partner there and in course of time became Lord Mayor of London and a Knight. It was he who invited Philippa and me to the Ball at the HAC in 1950 where we became engaged!

In 1986 when I retired as a Senior Partner we were around 350 people and 40 Partners and were one of the larger firms in the City. It was only in the 1990s that the absurdly large firms of over 1,000 people developed.

An Articled Clerk had to know his way round the City, not only by road, but through buildings. Our buildings at Copthall Avenue were a huge affair with many different entrances and addresses according to the entrance used. It was one of the passageways used by everyone in the City for speedy transit. For instance, through this and other buildings one could quickly get from Copthall Avenue to the Stock Exchange, the Bank of England, Old Broad Street, Bishopsgate and other quite remote locations if one knew how. This was one of the first things one had to learn! In some of the corridors there were shops to supply such passers-by, including on our ground floor. After some years I introduced on our first floor a free coffee machine for our staff. This got round the City and queues stretching round the building started to form for free coffee. We had to change the location!

An Articled Clerk started with menial jobs like sorting dividend vouchers for Trust account preparation and graduated to sitting with a Manager to learn Conveyancing, Litigation, Trusts and Company and Commercial Law. Most of the Managers were good masters and I started with a Mr Crocket in Conveyancing who was a great talker and very able. I remember he was paid £800 per annum which was then the going rate. I went the usual rounds of the Office and then went to Law School in Lancaster Gate prior to taking the Final Solicitors Exam.

Different firms had different systems for dealing with Articled Clerks who prior to the war had to pay a premium for being articled. I believe ours was one of the most expensive at around £1,000. This was the context in which towards the end of the war, having been wounded in Normandy, Willie Pybus approached Freshfields (one of the leading firms) to enquire about being articled after the war. He saw one of the Senior Partners and the question of premium was raised. Willie rather pressed for a decision as to taking him, but the Partner said, 'My boy, you would be unwise to commit yourself now. After all, last time you were only wounded!'.

We had an outstanding reputation for the quality of our training and almost anyone who had been articled to us was able to get the best jobs. Our alumni thus came to run quite a number of leading firms and institutions. For instance when I was on a Committee of the House of Lords years later, dealing with finance and the City, by far the best evidence given by the head of the City body dealing with this was our ex-Articled Clerk. The Insurance Ombudsman had the same background. When eventually many of our people went to Denton Hall and they decided to join up with a well-known firm – Wilde Sapte – their Managing Partner who negotiated the deal and who became a Managing Partner of the joint firm was similarly from our stable.

The firm had inevitably lost many clients during the war as there was such a strong international element. It recovered rapidly after 1950 when my father rejoined after resigning as Minister of Civil Aviation. The Jewish connection of the firm had always been strong, but after the war many of the leading businesses were developed by members of the Jewish Community and many of these came to the firm which came to be known as the leading Jewish firm. Essentially the basis of practice was contact with people for whom we acted in their personal affairs and incidentally for their businesses. Many of these businesses became very successful and the work we did in this connection outweighed what we did for them personally – though we continued to do that. An outstanding example was the Sainsbury family and their business which we floated on the Stock Exchange and who were our most important clients. But there were others who developed in this way such as the Clark family, and Plessey which became one of the foremost electronic and defence companies and was eventually acquired by GEC.

The clients became friends and I found the personal contacts rewarding. I never had an 'institutional' client where I was dealing with, effectively, a civil servant as client. This might have happened when I was dealing with ICI property, particularly their HQ in Millbank. This came about from a long connection. In the 1920s my father came to know the Mond family who founded ICI, as I have mentioned elsewhere, and he started to act for them in their personal and business matters. We continued to act for them personally for many years and I had much to do with them. However, not surprisingly in the 1920s ICI went for their commercial work to firms then better known than HON&V with the exception of this property work. So I did this for many years, and got to know and like the head of the property department well – Rutherford Warren. His son became articled to me and went off fairly shortly after qualifying to one of the banks to be an internal legal adviser. In time ICI decided to deal with their property work in-house.

I was never a property expert but had some interesting property experiences. For instance I sold Amen House for the Oxford University Press when it was bought for use as an extension of the Old Bailey. With a client I was involved in the development of a new village which was to incorporate 'Granny houses' of one room which at that time was a new idea. That I found exciting. Then there was the use of property, for revival as public entertainment, of an eighteenth-century club devoted to devil worship. Entertainment Tax at that time was in force and the authorities sought to tax the owner on this. I had to argue that devil worship was a religious activity outside the scope of the tax. Fortunately the tax was abolished before this came to court!

Then there was the client in the 1960s who had a country home and power lines were to be erected on his land. Long before concern arose as to health effects of emissions of electric and magnetic fields from these (as it did, perhaps without foundation, in the 1990s) the client suggested as an argument that these lines would make him impotent. Since he already had four children I told him that perhaps this would be a good thing! At any rate I put this to the electricity authority and we had a good-humoured correspondence ending in the erection of the lines, not to our surprise. The client had no more children.

There were other unusual experiences. One I remember when I was advising a client I knew very well on his company and we came upon a problem to which we could find no solution. When I was having a bath that evening I thought it through and found the solution. Next day I told him of all this and he was delighted with the result of my bath. He and I went shortly afterwards to his bankers and were discussing company matters when again we came upon a problem which none of us could think of a way of resolving. In this great gathering in the Banking Hall which echoed to all corners, my client announced that he thought I should take another bath!

Generally I made it a rule not to go to the States for less than a week because of jet lag. However, a new client asked me to go urgently to Rochester, New York and the fee was attractive. Although it was only for a couple of days, I decided to go. The job involved urgently drafting some long and complicated Patent-related documents on which the client and his American lawyer were also working. We sat up until late drafting until the client and his lawyer decided to pack in from exhaustion. I was very tired, but had very limited time to complete the job and so carried on. I had recently been to a health farm – Forest Mere – at Liphook and there had been introduced to yoga. I was hopeless at the exercises, but appreciated the system and the relaxation of body and mind we were taught. I decided this was the occasion to try out relaxation. I went to my bedroom and did as I was instructed to relax, and an hour later got up refreshed and finished the job to the astonishment of the client who felt shamefaced to have retired so early!

I was instructed by the Learned Societies to seek a way in which subscriptions could be made under covenant, the effect of which would be advantageous in relation to tax and thus help the Societies and perhaps their members. To establish this case three Learned Societies were selected – the British Academy, the Society of Antiquaries and a Trust of the Royal Engineers. But to return to the case. It was to come before the Special Commissioners of Income Tax (a sort of Tax court) and I instructed a Counsel who was a tax specialist. We went to visit the clients and he provided the transport. I was impressed by his stable of cars. We went to the Royal Engineers in Chatham in a Jaguar and to the Special Commissioners in a hearse-like Austin six-seater. It was only afterwards that I learnt he did not have a car, but hired what he thought appropriate to the occasion!

The point at issue was that the Revenue contended that the members had the benefit of receipt of the journal and this disqualified them from using a covenant for payment – with its advantageous tax consequences. Even free tea would disqualify them! I produced *Archaeologia* – the Journal of the Antiquaries – and we argued that nobody could understand this other than an expert, and that membership was confined to the experts. So the Society was exercising its charitable function by providing members with the journals, not conferring a benefit on them. We won and so these Societies were – and still are – able to have subscriptions under covenant!

I came to know Mortimer Wheeler, the great television character who really put archaeology on the map, through this and it was he and the owner and Chairman of Butterworths, the Law Publishers, who proposed me for membership of the Athenaeum. Years later Butterworths asked me to write a major work on Charity Law, but I declined partly because I was ill-qualified, but mostly because it would have been a lifetime tie with constant revision.

The connection led in time to my being asked by the Foundation for Science & Technology (which acted to help Learned Societies in formal and legal matters) to address the Learned Societies, which I did, and in due course to become a Member of the Foundation.

I attended many of their lectures and discussions when I was in the House of Lords chairing the Environment Committee and later as a member of the Science and Technology Committee. It provides a welcome means of keeping in touch with many old friends.

Whilst the firm had a substantial property practice and many experts in the field, I was never one of them. In the early years I was chiefly concerned with Trusts which I found interesting and intellectually stimulating. Of course most of the work was in creating and seeing to the administration of them. Sometimes, however, questions arose which had to go to the courts.

Selection of Counsel in this as in all other fields is an essential function of a solicitor. Of course expertise in the law is essential. But there are some who get unnerved if the client is less than honest or indeed a crook – and alas some are, even if they are on the winning side in the case in question. Some Counsel are good at cross-examination and some bad – particularly if they have no confidence in the client. So selection of the right person is important.

One of the first cases I had involved reference to a Compensation Commission to claim for property lost due to action in an enemy territory during the war. There were quite a number of these Commissions, most inadequately funded to provide even reasonable compensation for these losses, and the law involved was usually difficult and complicated. I decided I had to instruct either a leading QC, or a very inexperienced barrister whom the Members of the Commission might feel they should help out of sympathy! I instructed Tony Barrowclough, then newly called to the Bar. The Members of the Commission seeing this novice opposed by experienced Counsel gave him help (as is usual in courts by judges too in such cases). We won!

Then there was a case of a Trust in which a very senior QC had been involved, whom I thought quite useless. The dispute was between beneficiaries and the Trustees had little part to play, but the Trustees had to be represented in court. So I instructed the QC on behalf of the Trustees and thus kept him silent, instructing good Juniors to act for the warring parties!

Of course Counsel advise in conference as well as appearing in court and one learns a lot from them. For instance there was Irvine Goulding (later a judge) who used to take one through the problem step by step and reach a conclusion, and I learnt a great deal from him. I asked him how he came to be such a wonderful teacher and he told me in the war he had been a Naval Instructor. Others equally good in the law would often apparently leap to a conclusion and one had no idea how or why.

There was an amazing case in which I was instructed by the Trustees, who were spread around the world, of Trusts created by a very successful German Jewish businessman who died in Paris leaving a son. Following the death of his father, the son arranged the funeral in Paris, summoning the Trustees to attend which they did. As the coffin was being lowered into the grave, the son served proceedings upon them across it. Disputes and litigation continued for years and at one time in twenty-one different jurisdictions simultaneously. Some German law of the utmost complexity arose on which I had to take advice of a professor at the leading institute in Hamburg, who took a year to produce his opinion. This was couched in such obscure language that I had to ask a professor in Cambridge to translate, which he did after some six months of hard labour.

In time it became clear that these disputes must be settled and so the son found a man willing to attempt this. He submitted his travelling expense accounts regularly to the son. On one occasion he thought the cost of travel for one person to Brussels seemed excessive, so he looked into the matter and found it was not a fare to Brussels, but for two to Corsica – for the intermediary and the son's wife. Shortly after this the whole matter was settled!

There was an extraordinary case arising from an attack by the European Commission on the World Aluminium Industry. Our British client was involved and the Russian industry was also attacked. The Russians did not at that time recognise the existence of the Community and a fine levied against them would have raised the most difficult political consequences. At that time the Commission acted both as prosecutor and judge in such cases. I believed that the Commission could not impose a fine on the Russians even if they found all the defendants guilty – including our client. It seemed to me that we could argue that it would be contrary to all notions of justice that one defendant alone should be excused from paying a penalty; so if the Russians were not to be fined neither should we be. I discovered that if there were a five-year delay in imposing a penalty none could thereafter be imposed. So I waited with bated breath for expiration of the five years, and four days after it expired received a formal notice saying that whilst our clients were guilty, no fine would in the circumstances be imposed. This case was of course extensively reported in the Law Reports.

Practice of the law is supposed to be dull, but I never found it so. Generally I was keen to be ahead of the game and embarked on fields which never matured into an effective basis for practice. For instance on a visit to Sheffield I arranged for a great expert in Labour Law to join us as a consultant following Barbara Castle's White Paper on the subject, 'In Place of Strife'. On the introduction of VAT I made quite a study of it. After creation of the European Community I did a lot of work on that and later engaged as part of our staff a Member of the Commission staff to educate us and deal with cases. In none of these instances did anything useful emerge. One can easily be too far ahead of the game! Indeed in the early 1970s I was consulted by some Swiss clients on investing in office property in the City, which I advised against because values would go down due to lack of demand following development of the Internet. How wrong I was! On the other hand, I arranged for Professor Wheatcroft to join us as a consultant on tax, he being a leading expert and having written the leading books; and this was a success.

Many solicitors take on non-executive directorships of companies. But I rarely did, partly because a company is run by executive directors and one never knows what is happening unless and until disaster strikes – then one is accused of failing in one's duty!

In my late thirties I was approached by Martin Schaull whom I must have met at the CBF (Central British Fund for Jewish Relief and Rehabilitation) to join the Board of JW French & Co. Ltd, a private company of which he was Managing Director and which belonged to and was chaired by a Mr French. When I saw him I liked him and he looked as if he was ex-Army. He accepted me, but said privately to Martin, 'He is a bit young, isn't he?' It was a very high-class flour milling company operating mainly at Chelsea Flour Mills next to Lots Road Power Station. We supplied top level companies like Floris who were specialist high-grade patissiers and our main customer was Lyons. Martin was a good chemist as well as running the company well. He had a long-standing friend, Andrew Haas, who was one of the nicest human beings I have met, very able particularly on the finance side, and came from Czechoslovakia as a refugee as had Martin. Later Henry Cohen joined the company and brought considerable flour business and business ability. I remained a Director for quite a time and learnt a lot about flour and old 'undershot and overshot' mill wheels. I never really understood the business and made, I felt, little contribution, but I enjoyed the experience and the friendships made. The company had a cash and carry business in Chichester run by a Mr Huntingdon. As a Director I was able to use it. In time Mr Huntingdon left to take over running a grocer's in Birdham and the business was disposed of. He took on running the shop at Chichester Yacht Basin so I had a friend there! Later he started a wine shop in a barn in Appledram where I found a Jeroboam of champagne which I bought for some future special occasion. Years later it supplied Jenny's party at the Orangery in Holland Park (The Belvedere Restaurant) for celebration of getting her degree.

The firm had long acted for Manpower, an American company with a UK subsidiary of some importance, and I was asked to be a Director in succession to Eric Wolff, one of our Partners. I found this a great experience because the company was embarking on what was then a new approach to employment. Its purpose was to provide really well-trained staff (who were Manpower employees) long- or short-term for almost any job. It had its own arrangements for training staff where necessary. The company acquired such a reputation that many companies came to it for really good people, perhaps to undertake a short-term specialised job for which they had no suitable staff – and it would have been absurd for them to undertake it themselves. For instance, at one time there were many large flotations of companies on the Stock Exchange which had to be handled by the big banks. For this they required a large team of experienced people trained in the job, which would only last a few weeks. We supplied them. Unusually we provided the chief engineer for a few years' appointment at Lerwick oil terminal when it originally opened. For a spell we provided the management for Dyce Airport, the main base for North Sea oil at the time. The job was carefully assessed by the company and it was their expertise and care in this as well as assessment of those chosen to fill the jobs that gave the company its high reputation. Our general employment reports and assessments were highly regarded and reported regularly in the national press.

The President and main driving force of this remarkable development was an unassuming man called Mitchel Fromstein, and the HQ was in Milwaukee. When the Managing Director in the UK retired to do other things the remaining Directors stayed in office, but I was asked to seek out a new chief man. I sought advice and found a number of possible candidates with high-powered experience and sent the list to Fromstein. He rejected them all and decided to appoint Lillian Bennett, who was one of the Directors, as Chairman. I confess this had not occurred to me and I believe Fromstein felt that he could get on with her and might have personal trouble with the people I had recommended. He was right! She made a great success of the job and the company prospered greatly under her. We became friends and after her retirement – and mine – we remain so.

Then there was Goldbergs. One of my father's oldest clients was IW Goldberg, whom I think he knew before the First World War in the context of East End Boys' Clubs. He had a family timber firm which he ran with a rod of iron – pretty successfully. For many years he had a Manager there, Stanley Philips, who was very knowledgeable and conscientious, but whom IW never allowed to run anything. From an early stage I looked after the legal side of the company and the family Trusts IW set up after the Second World War. At that time people who had private companies set up Trusts for tax reasons; they were very effective and I dealt with a lot of them. So I knew IW pretty well and we were on good terms, he being slightly younger than my father.

To my astonishment and alarm I learnt after his death that he had written a note to say he wanted me to be Chairman of the company until his nephew Paul, whom he treated as his heir (he being unmarried) was fit to take over. Paul was the son of IW's brother living in South Africa who had no knowledge of the timber business – and nor had I! So, under the close and friendly guidance of Mr Philips, we continued the business. Paul was intelligent, but I was not happy that he should take charge of the direction of the company.

There was the main company, Y Goldberg & Sons in Uxbridge, Clarks Wood in Bristol and another dormant company in Manchester. They had a steady business which we maintained. IW had been well known in the trade and had been President of the Timber Trades Federation. He was successful in acquiring customers and suppliers and developed a connection with Israel where his contacts had access to timber in West Africa and manufactured high-quality plywood which was a mainstay of the business. Softwood and ply also came from Finland and hardwood from Singapore. It was an interesting business to be in, but with Mr Philips about to retire we had to find a successor and were very fortunate in finding Ron Lewis in Bristol. A company Secretary – Mr Moss – was appointed, and a young trainee who eventually became a Director. I enjoyed this Directorship and of course as Chairman I knew what was happening. In time Ron Lewis succeeded Mr Philips and moved the HQ of the companies to Bristol.

During this period the company asked me to go to Finland twice to secure contracts there. Philippa and I went and thoroughly enjoyed our time and meeting the Finns. We saw a lot of the country and at one place we visited to see suppliers, we were interviewed by the press who next day had a banner headline, 'The Lord comes to – '! We went to the Arctic Circle to Rovaniemi, and saw trees being floated down the river and met reindeer whom we thought looked very sad and humourless – perhaps because of the long dark winters which they, unlike the inhabitants who go south to warmer climes, cannot avoid! We twice went to Singapore, Malaysia and Indonesia because the tax regime there had altered so that it was no longer good to buy from Singapore. Indonesia and Malaysia wanted, quite reasonably, to make the money from converting timber into plywood rather than allowing Singapore to get this trade and profit. I saw the Government in Jakarta and was told that they were building a hundred ply mills to achieve this; I suggested that was far too many, but they went ahead. Of course with demand for hardwood a lot of the ancient forests were being clear-felled and in theory the Government gave grants to the local people to replant on grounds of 'sustainability'. Increase in population resulted in much of this cleared land being converted to agriculture which was more profitable and I was told with derision about the purpose of the grants which were pocketed by the recipients. I believed it!

In Sumatra we were looked after by Goldberg friends who were ethnic Chinese and extremely able, and they took us from the capital, Medan, up a road towards Ace which is said to be the last refuge of the white elephant. The road is on an embankment not quite wide enough to allow two vehicles to pass and as the drivers are unforgiving, death is a regular consequence of using the road. Fortunately we survived. Back at the capital our hosts gave us an excellent Chinese meal and then invited us to see nightlife. We sat on the pavement of a busy street along the side of which were numerous stalls selling cooked and uncooked food and drink. Washing up was done in the gutter. We had to choose something so we confined ourselves to tea in the hope that boiling water (if indeed it was boiling) would save us from infection. We survived that too.

I invited our hosts to contact us when in London so that we could reciprocate. This they did, but brought the whole family of some twenty people and we had to take a whole restaurant in Covent Garden to entertain them!

Another Chinese family in Kuching in Sarawak looked after us there in splendid style and we had the chance of going into the jungle and 'longhouses'. It was a great experience. Apparently a gathering of the Heads of the States of the Federation took place there and in order to impress them the local Government laid on a Rolls Royce for each which they kept afterwards! There is a magnificent building in the city with a gold roof to show its wealth. We kept in touch with the family for many years through Christmas cards.

On mainland Malaysia we were entertained by a Goldberg contact in Kuala Lumpur who drove us at breakneck speed up a twisting road to the Heights where there was a splendid hotel and restaurant and other facilities. Philippa was made to feel very ill by this trip and when sea slugs were produced for lunch this finished her off. It was later with another contact that we had freshwater shrimps which made her very ill. We had an interesting time but had to survive a variety of perils!

Throughout our stay we had had only Chinese food. When we

returned to Singapore a very rich Chinese business man took us to the leading hotel and gave us a European meal which included a steak and profiterole – all excellent. However we found it so heavy after three weeks of Chinese cuisine that we felt quite ill.

It was on this occasion that there was a legal meeting of the International Bar Association at which I was to address the gathering on some environmental subject and close the meeting. There for the first time I met John Salter, a Partner in Denton Hall whom I later came to know well. Lord McKay, who later became Lord Chancellor, was opening the meeting which I was closing and knowing little of environmental matters, asked my help. That was how I came to know and admire him.

On another occasion kind friends asked us out on their motor boat in the harbour and we had lunch on board. We were to return so that I could join a cocktail party with the other lawyers. Our host missed the tide and we had to wade ashore. I had been told that Singapore was free of pollution, but I found that the oil had sunk and was covered in it up to my thighs as I emerged. It was in this condition that I appeared at the hotel where everyone was assembling to depart for the party. There was after all no purpose in covering it up and thus ruining one's clothes! Chairmanship of Goldbergs had many facets.

It soon became clear that if any of Paul's inheritance was to be saved the company would have to be sold – and this was no great sorrow to Paul. I discussed this with Ron Lewis who expressed an interest in buying and I sent him off to other solicitors to be advised. He bought, and so Paul's financial position was crystallised and the future of the company came into able hands. It prospered. I was asked to open the new HQ building in Bristol and a plaque commemorates the occasion. Happily I have remained in touch with Ron.

I had become Senior Partner of the firm in 1978 when Leslie Cork retired from that position, which he had held since my father's death in 1963. The firm had prospered over this period and he did much to modernise the firm. For instance he introduced what had become common practice among City firms – time recording for the purpose of assessing bills. Of course I submitted to this but was never enthusiastic as so much else in addition to time had to be considered.

He saw to the introduction of computerised accounting, which was essential, and the appointment of a high-powered Chief Accountant. I was left with much responsibility for staff, which I enjoyed. When I became Senior Partner I arranged for other Partners to do much of the general administration and accounting, but continued with most staff matters. We had staff parties at home most years, as my father had, and consumption of food was prodigious! We provided perhaps four alternative main dishes, but they ate the lot on one plate. It was great fun and we all enjoyed ourselves. Interestingly very little alcohol was ever drunk and I never recall any drunkenness at our home parties or others, such as annual office parties or anniversary celebrations such as 'fifty years with the firm'.

I was exceptionally fortunate in having a car and driver at my disposal and at first after my father's death Len Chandler continued with me. Then it was decided it would be better if he were available for other Partners and I should have someone else. Chandler was a great character with a wonderful fund of stories which he told with immense vigour and humour. One of the best was how he was asked by one of our Partners to collect the ashes of a client and well-known comic actor and to take them to another solicitor's office. He put the casket beside him and carried on a conversation with him on the journey (which Chandler recounted at length) and then delivered the package to the girl at reception, who asked what it contained. When told she passed out!

I had another driver who drove so violently that when a new car was required I got a diesel Peugeot which was one of the toughest one could buy. But not tough enough, as I found when the engine stopped in the city and we called the AA who decreed it would have to be replaced.

And then Patrick appeared, an Irishman with a great sense of humour. He had apparently spent many years on the west coast of the USA and at one time represented Rolls Royce, whose cars he sold to the film stars. He seems to have had his own aeroplane so must have been doing well. He went into property and at one time while living in Los Angeles was working in Texas so had to commute weekly which was expensive. By a happy chance he saw in a newspaper an advertisement for an airline that took 'reverends' for free; and by an even better chance in the same edition that degrees in Divinity could be acquired for a few dollars. This he promptly did and, donning a dog collar, travelled for free for the rest of his time there!

He has a sister who is a nun and was responsible for the interdenominational church established at Milton Keynes. She organised a party of nuns to visit the holy places in Israel and Patrick joined the party. I can imagine that he electrified the members! While in Galilee he picked up a bug and came home in a bad way – so bad that, after I had sent him privately to a Harley Street specialist, he was advised that he could not continue to drive professionally. He retired, to my great regret.

Miss Duce retired after thirty-three years with me in 1983 and of course this was a great sadness because she was outstanding in all she did; she knew the history of every matter over so long a time – and the people too. So our Queen Bee had to look for another secretary for me and eventually found a remarkable lady who had marvellous shorthand and typing, a degree, was highly intelligent and spoke fluent French and Italian which was a great asset as I was doing much international work at the time. I met her and was greatly impressed, but was concerned at her red hair and said so to our Queen Bee, half in jest! I was only too right. She had a very strong personality and experienced Partners quaked as she appeared at their door. I myself never had a row with her, but she had upset a number of people in the office and clearly she had to go and I think she realised this too.

While she was with me I was asked to give a lecture in Paris in French on Trusts and Taxation, which I originally wrote out in French and she corrected; it was wonderful to have someone who could do this. In preparation for the lecture I had some visual aids prepared showing in diagrammatic form how various elements of Trusts worked and the tax consequences. At the lecture the French tax authorities were represented and I had great fun in watching them copying out these slides and then removing them at the crucial moment. I do not think they learnt much of use to them!

A replacement secretary had to be found and Alex came on the scene. Physically she was very small. She was highly intelligent, had a degree and first-class secretarial skills. She was much liked in the office which was important because as secretary to the Junior Partner she had much influence on the smooth and happy running of the firm. Having married she went on deferred honeymoon to Kenya and there suffered a very severe accident and broke her back. She was out of action for a long time and I had temporary assistance. After she returned she had to have her back re-broken and reset which meant another long absence. Eventually she was to start a family and decided rightly in my view to leave – to my great regret. She was active when I lost my sight and was an enormous help and moral support in very difficult circumstances. I had realised early on that there were defects in my sight when in Singapore for the Goldberg company, because I could not read the notices in the airport. Another time I was sailing back from Flushing after a sailing holiday in Holland and everything was going fine – we were drifting west with the tide as planned and not far off Newhaven when one of the crew quietly suggested we go about and he told me there was an enormous tanker approaching. The weather was clear, but despite my best efforts, I never saw it. Fortunately I did as advised. I decided the time had come for action on my sight.

In November 1984 I had my first cataract operation and I well remember immediately after release from hospital, when wearing very dark glasses, I was requested to attend a Partners' meeting at the office which I reluctantly did. There were clearly stresses in the Partnership which I should have acted on, but this was impossible and I well remember Iko Meshoulam kindly taking me by the arm to guide me out of the room when the meeting was over as I could not see a thing. As the other eye had a cataract too I could not read – and this went on for around two years. Alex was marvellous in reading things for me as was Mary, my Clerk, in the House of Lords. When I had to open a debate in the House following completion of one of the Reports from Committees which I had chaired, Alex wrote out my notes in huge letters so that I could read them. It was an extremely difficult time. In January 1986 I had the second cataract operation and suffered a cardiac arrest due to a failure of the anaesthetic system. I remember I awoke in intensive care with Philippa, who had been summoned, and decided there and then to give up smoking!

I had not had the cataract operation and I was furious and requested that it be done – which it was, under local anaesthetic.

Gradually I could see more, but the after-effects of the cardiac arrest resulted in clinical depression which went on for a long time; indeed it was only when Barbara Clayton at a meeting of the Royal Commission on Environmental Pollution told me that it would take a year to recover that I started to get over the depression.

In October 1986 there was a meeting of the American Bar Association in Atlanta, at which I was scheduled to lecture on environmental law, and the firm were anxious I should go there. I did not enjoy it and found myself years older than most others there and got even more depressed! I had been unable to read effectively for some two years and so was out of touch with case law, let alone current developments through the Journals. On my return I decided to retire immediately as Senior Partner and later as Partner, which I did in April 1987.

By this time Alex had gone and had been replaced by Caroline, who was well educated and knew a bit about computers which was helpful. Patrick who had by then become my driver frequently brought her to Collyers, and on the way there and back had to stop once or more to buy sticky buns for her to eat! She had a considerable knowledge of history and used to spend weekends re-enacting historical events at stately homes open to the public which she greatly enjoyed. She told me she was a witch and I did not entirely disbelieve her.

When I was preparing the first Garner Lecture established by the UK Environmental Law Association I wanted to quote earlier instances of the social consequences of radical changes in agriculture and mentioned this to her. Next day she produced exactly the quotation I wanted from Sir Thomas More's *Utopia* from the early sixteenth century!

I decided on retiring as Senior Partner that I must leave my room which I had inherited from my father as it would be easier for my successor. Caroline was involved in the depressing task of disposing of many books and pictures and furniture which belonged to me. *Hansards* went to London University whilst the prints which decorated much of the office were sold. They came from my father who had

had not only the most important collection of books on London in private hands, but also of prints, many of which were in the office. I retained a very few which I still have.

I moved to the second floor where we had space and stayed there for the rest of my time. It was then that I was advised to have a computer – one in the office and an identical one at home and I was put in touch with our computer consultants to select the right system. They chose a Wang which did me very well for many years. Caroline showed me around it and I had one day of instruction from a teacher. I learnt much – indeed when eventually I went to Denton Hall I was to be seen instructing my secretary there how to use a computer!

In 1988 Philippa lost her hearing and I put in a fax machine at home and another in the office so that she could communicate if in trouble. I still have the fax machine then bought and it works perfectly!

Of course being remote from the rest of the firm I became out of touch with developments, but rumours reached me of trouble. The firm was doing as well as it ever had in terms of business and profits, but there were increasingly severe rows between Partners. There was nothing I could do having retired as a Partner and being so remote from the firm. Eventually the firm split up, by dissolution of the Partnership which seemed to me a mad thing to do. I was particularly anxious to secure the future pensions of those who had retired and those who had yet to do so. My main concern was for staff, but of course I was personally interested also.

The outcome, as a result of the great and skilled efforts principally of John Rosenheim and Iko Meshoulam, was that the bulk of the firm was merged with Denton Hall whilst the disaffected group of Partners joined Richards Butler and others joined other firms.

We were received in a very friendly way by the Partners and staff of Denton Hall. I had a room looking onto a well in a very modern air-conditioned building far different from our old one. Originally a secretary who had been for many years with a Denton Hall Partner and who had now partly retired was allocated to me. She had imagined that I might have a couple of letters to do each day but as we continued our discussion and it was clear that I was likely to be very busy, she said she could not possibly do it and we parted – as we remained – on the friendliest terms! Julia Vince was then allocated to me and remained throughout my time there. Secretaries were housed in cubicles off the corridor outside the boss's office, which I had not seen before, but they seemed to think the arrangement satisfactory.

Denton Hall had a very similar attitude to practice to ours and were very generous to our staff who had retired and had pensions, which relieved me a lot. John Salter was very anxious that I should be in his group and develop the environmental law side of the practice which at that time was a novelty.

I had just recently finished the Royal Commission study of Genetically Modified Organisms and somehow the BBC must have heard of my interest in it as they contacted me at the office, said they wanted to do a television programme and would set up a studio in the basement! They did and this caused great excitement and I think put me on the map there. BBC Radio also did interviews with me, but these were in my room and caused less commotion.

Julie had no experience of computers and as I wanted to continue my arrangements with one at home and one in the office, I gave her some instruction, as mentioned earlier, which caused amusement and amazement!

A number of staff spent time on environmental matters though at that time there was not much paying work in this field, which has since developed as one of the key fields of law in which to be in practice. One of those who came from Australia was Glen McLeod who worked with me a lot and returned after several years to Perth where, when we went there, he and his family were wonderful hosts to Philippa and me. He had become a Partner in one of the leading firms dealing with environmental matters, so I was rather proud he had been a pupil of mine!

CHAPTER FIVE

Charities, Environment and Other Interests

AFTER I HAD QUALIFIED I felt I should play some part in Anglo-Jewish activity and, following my term as Warden of Berkeley Street, was glad when asked to stand for election to the Board of Deputies of British Jews, the elected representative body of Anglo-Jewry. Plenary meetings were on Sundays once a month which was a bore, but possible as we were then living in London.

At that time the overwhelming majority of Jews were enthusiastic Zionists and this was reflected on the Board. On formation of the State of Israel it took over from the British Mandate which had run Palestine since the first War. Whilst the idea of the State was reflected in the Balfour Declaration – a British initiative – the post-War British Government was hostile, particularly the Foreign Office and the Foreign Secretary Ernest Bevin. It was remarkable that the new State was well thought-of among people generally in the UK and this was largely achieved by wonderful sensitivity of the Israelis in their choice of Ambassador, Mr Eliash, a saintly and strict Orthodox Jew who maintained an extreme Kosher diet without show, and was a modest and undemonstrative man. Therefore despite possibilities of great hostility, Israel was well regarded.

The difficulty at the Board which I found was that the members there thought they ought to be running Israel and were highly critical of the Israeli Government. I found this situation absurd. I was on the Foreign Affairs Committee of the Board and there I found the same in more extreme degree. Members were effectively 'professional Jews' who were immensely knowledgeable in all things Jewish and Zionist, but in my view almost always wrong (ignorant as I was).

'My old nose', as I used to say to my father who approved of instinct in the absence of knowledge, 'told me so'. And I suppose that having been to and advised the Israeli Government I in fact knew more than most of those pontificating at the Board. I came to the conclusion that the Zionists did more harm to the cause of Israel than those opposed to them! As a result of all this I resigned from the Board.

Then somehow I came in touch with the CBF (the Central British Fund for Jewish Relief and Rehabilitation). It had been formed in 1933 to deal with the German Jewish refugee problems which were then just starting. A remarkable woman, Joan Stiebel, became its first Secretary appointed by the founders, the Schiff family. It was heavily supported by the Anglo-Jewish community and all its main pillars. As the problems increased so did its activity until it became in effect the main body responsible for receiving Jewish refugees from Germany and trusted by the Home Office. One of the great characters at that time, and later when I became involved, was Oscar Joseph, one of three brothers who ran a merchant bank in the City – Leopold Joseph. By an extraordinary chance John Quicke's son Michael became and still is its Managing Director.

Oscar was a man of whom Prince Albert would have approved – absolutely straight and bound by a very strict moral code in all he did – including telling the truth rather than using evasive fibs to slide over difficulties. He thus became unpopular in some circles, but I found him a wonderful person to work with.

In the late fifties, when I became involved, the German Jewish affairs were dealt with by a Jewish Refugees Committee separate from the then current activities of the CBF. These included a number of homes for elderly refugees – and many of them were old by then. Others had of course been assimilated into the Anglo-Jewish Community or gone to the USA.

The main concerns when I started were for Jews in Eastern Europe and Arab countries. As to the former, little could be done for those in Russia as they were not allowed to leave and all that could be done was to send parcels which provided food or were saleable items which thus provided money. Those comparatively few Jews who were in Poland were in time able to leave and they went by a route via Austria and Italy; some went to Israel, others to the USA and elsewhere. I went to Vienna and saw Mr Kreisky who held high office there and expressed admiration for the arrangements made for transit of the Poles, some of whom I saw arriving by train.

Far larger numbers were involved in Arab countries from which they wished to emigrate to Israel, which had of course an open-door policy for all Jews. We worked closely with the American Joint Distribution Committee particularly in Morocco where there were about 300,000 Jews. The King – Hassan – was not unhelpful provided publicity was not given to the Jewish emigration and our activities there, so we had to work quietly and in the end without any fuss they all left, mostly for Israel. The result was satisfactory, but absence of publicity meant great difficulty in raising funds in the UK. I was Treasurer and that was my main function so I was particularly conscious of the problem.

I went to Morocco a couple of times; once was to see the work of associate bodies dealing with health, in which no distinction was made between Jew and Arabs as regards availability of treatment in the clinics. Much of the work related to blindness and scalp infection and was very successful. On another occasion several of us including Joan Stiebel went on a trip covering Tangier, Casablanca, Fez, Meknes and Marrakech in four days and we had about four hours' sleep altogether! It was a particularly interesting time as the UN had started a programme of assisting local people to establish their own economy, including growing crops, rather than sending food which had been the practice. This is now common practice, but not then. In the Atlas Mountains we met a young rabbi of a small community who had been trained at a Yeshiva in Gateshead, which was odd as this was an Ashkenazi institution whereas of course the locals were Sephardic. In Marrakech we lay on sofas on our right side and plucked chicken from the bone, and ate couscous with our left hand as is the Arab custom.

The Council of the CBF was so old that in accordance with English Company Law, resolutions had to be passed annually at the Annual General Meeting authorising those over seventy – and that was everyone – to be elected!

To raise money I started a CBF Annual Ball held at the Dorchester Hotel and managed to get this recognised in the Community as one

1960 Worshipful Company of Gardeners visit to King Baudouin Laerkin Palace, Brussels. Schweder, Steiner, Beadle, the author, Sheran, Talbot, Thornton-Smith, Kerman, Lymbury, Howard, Gardner, Gollin.

of the great social events of the season. So everyone who was anyone came. On one occasion I remember having arranged a menu ending with a special ice-cream dish highly decorated and lit with candles. All the lights were extinguished as the waiters came in carrying the dishes high. At the point of their entrance a carpet must have been rucked up as one after another they fell to the ground spilling their precious cargo with particular effect on a lady who was much disliked, to the pleasure of all present – except her!

We had a raffle at the Ball every year. After three years I retired as Chairman of the Ball, but thereafter of course attended with a party. On one such occasion after I had retired we won the major prize which was a cruise of the Caribbean given by Chandris Lines. Had I been Chairman I must have felt bound to surrender it, but as it was we kept it and went on the cruise. What a win!

Meantime I had become a Liveryman of the Worshipful Company of Gardeners through the interest of my father. This is one of the ancient Guilds founded around 1340 to see to the maintenance of high standards in the sale of garden produce 'within the City and six miles thereof'. It operated a system of licensing and thus acquired a monopoly of the grant of permission to sell and, as in all ages, this gave them power and money. They became very rich and when James I came to the throne and was short of cash, he agreed to authorise continuation of the Company's rights provided it became a Chartered Company at a substantial fee. Thus the Company had its first Charter in 1606. Over the years it went into decline and was revived in the late nineteenth century as a charitable and social body largely interested in horticultural education and development in which it worked closely with the Royal Horticultural Society.

The Company holds about five dinners a year and in those days I used to attend most of them. One was to take place on 14 June 1952. Philippa was then expecting Jenny – and indeed was so expectant that I had delivered her to Westminster Hospital. In those days it was not the practice for husbands to be present at the birth, but to let the wife, under proper care, get on with it. Indeed, a television programme the other night on Queen Victoria showed how a number of courtiers were in the Palace awaiting the birth of a child to the Queen and one said to another how ridiculous it was, as if it were his own wife he would have gone to his club! So I went to the Dinner on HQS Wellington moored in the Thames and had just finished the soup when someone came to tell me Jenny had arrived. I went to the hospital and saw all was well and then returned to finish the meal. Nowadays that would be thought very improper!

When I joined, although its object was to promote horticulture and therefore should have welcomed as members people active in the trade, there was an old boy on the Court who despised 'the trade', so any applicant for membership thus connected was black-balled. Therefore it was decided that two blackballs and not one were required to exclude a candidate! We now have many distinguished members of 'the trade', including the Director of Kew!

In time I became a Member of the Court and we had expeditions every year to some garden in England or Wales, and went to Belgium for the Floralie Ghentoise, a great flower show, and had splendid dinners at the Pavilion Restaurant in Brussels! The Clerk of the

Company dealt with the administration and originally in my time there was a Mr Steele who was excellent and was involved in the history of the company. He was succeeded by Frank Steiner, a charming solicitor. In his time we were invited to meet the King of the Belgians – King Baudouin – at Laerkin Palace. He was a Liveryman along with a number of other Royalty. We arrived in Brussels with, among others, David Longman, a Liveryman who was a leading florist in the city and found that Frank had forgotten to bring our posies of sweet-smelling herbs 'to keep off offensive smells and odours', which was part of our uniform and originated because the sewers used to run down the streets. David contacted his friends in Brussels at a late hour and asked them to supply them and deliver them to the Palace in time for our visit. In the morning we drove up to the Palace and after waiting a short time a white van appeared just before we were due to meet the King and from the back posies were hurriedly handed to each of us. It was then we realised that we had bouquet garni including spring onions and as the time came to meet the King we were all in tears. Indeed the effect was so powerful that the King was overcome too! It made the party go. It also resulted in the King inviting us all to Buckingham Palace, when he came for a State visit with Queen Fabiola, so that we might meet without tears!

In 1963 I became Master and was installed just before my father died in October, so he had the satisfaction of seeing that. The Autumn Court Dinner (which in fact was, as usual, a Livery Dinner of over a hundred) was to take place a few days after he died and of course the question arose as to whether or not I should attend, on which I naturally consulted my mother. She thought I should and I did. As I arrived an elderly Member, who was a good friend of my father and totally deaf, enquired after him and I replied that sadly he had died earlier in the week. 'Oh,' he said, 'I am so glad'. I could do nothing but laugh! It only has to be compared with the experience of my mother who had cancer and went to a specialist who sent a bill within the month addressed to 'The Executors of Eleanor Lady Nathan'. Luckily she had a great sense of humour and we composed a suitable reply!

It was the custom at that time after dinner that two students of the Guildhall School of Music would 'oblige with a song' and they ended up with a duet. I felt it was laughable, so for the Ladies' Banquet which we held annually I decided to see the Director of the School and arrange for them to put on Manotti's 'The Telephone' which is a joke opera about women ceaselessly on the telephone and, though modern, tuneful. I also decided to be revolutionary in having Sauterne instead of port at the end of the meal. It was a disaster. Not a flicker of a smile at the opera which was very well done by the students, and the absence of port was treated as horrific.

I took three initiatives during my year. There was work on the history of the Company, the introduction of the City Festival of Flowers to run with the newly introduced City Arts Festival, and a scheme to develop the grading and presentation of vegetables for sale. The Festival of Flowers was an advance on the Company's annual windowbox competition introduced a couple of years previously by Edward Howard (later Lord Mayor). At that time vegetables were generally sold on open shelves in front of greengrocers' shops and they were straight from the farm, unscrubbed and with potatoes covered in earth. They were ungraded and so of all sizes. Plastic was not used as packaging nor anything else. I approached Marks & Spencer who were just starting food sales and Wye College, the agricultural farm of London University, both of whom were receptive of the idea. From these innocent beginnings emerged the gross over-use of chemicals to ensure uniformity of product and the over-packaging to provide long shelf life and cleanliness from all of which we now suffer. How far this all is from the simple ideas I had in mind. It certainly never occurred to me that what I was proposing would engender a return to 'organic farming'!

The Court had become overloaded with old members who were blocking the way for new entrants and as I was very young – forty-one – the Company was likely to be lumbered with me for far too long. So, with difficulty, I introduced the idea of Past Masters ceasing to be voting members of the Court ten years after being Master. These were to be called 'Senior Past Masters'. I got this through with some opposition and it is now generally adopted in the City.

Each year as I have said an expedition was made by the Company to a garden – sometimes near London and sometimes more distant

– for instance we had a wonderful visit to Bodnant in Wales one year. It seemed to me that a visit to the Savile Gardens near Windsor, which belong to the Queen, would be interesting. It is a privilege of the Company to present the bouquet to the Queen on the occasion of her Coronation and a replica on each anniversary. The presentation on the anniversary is done by the Master so my turn came, and I went to Buckingham Palace for the purpose. There I found myself alone with the Queen who could not have been more welcoming. I brought the conversation round to the Savile Garden and she readily agreed we could make the visit. It was very human of her to say in general conversation that she found it very difficult to remember the names of all the shrubs and plants and before an important visit would ensure that the labels were placed where she could see them so that she would not be caught out!

As Master I had to attend many functions, some in the daytime such as flower shows, and many in the evening such as Livery Dinners of other Companies where I had to make an 'after dinner speech'. This is a special art form in that unlike a lecture it must be short, and a sort of soufflé which may contain an idea, but must have no substance and must be given as if off the cuff and not read! It is in many ways more difficult to compose than a lecture.

I had for some time been on the Executive Committee of the British Empire Cancer Campaign. It changed its name to 'Cancer Research Campaign' by which it is now known. It was formed in 1923 to sponsor research into cancer and its cure and was not intended to carry out much research itself. That is how it continued to operate. By contrast the Imperial Cancer Research Fund carried on extensive research itself in its own laboratories. Among the members of the Executive of the CRC was Professor Ernst Chain, who had the Nobel Prize for discovery of penicillin and whom my father knew quite well. It was he who approached me about becoming Chairman of the Executive. Chairman of the Campaign was the Duke of Devonshire and he presided once a year at meetings of the Council.

I was of course greatly honoured to be asked to be Chairman, but it seemed to me then that there would be much advantage in an amalgamation of the Campaign and the Fund to reduce appeal costs and generally to be more effective and economical with one major national cancer charity. I also thought this would be well received by the public in that the number of appeals would be reduced. I made it a condition of taking on the Chairmanship that I should be at liberty to try and bring this about. There was some opposition, but eventually it was agreed.

A very distinguished surgeon, Dickson Wright, was then Chairman of the Fund. He was an impossibly difficult man as others warned me – and an excellent but very vulgar after-dinner speaker! I tried to meet him with a view to a discussion but this proved impossible and despite continual efforts I had to give up any idea of bringing the two together. It was said – and maybe rightly – that two appeals would bring in more money than one combined appeal. The comparison was not to be available in practice so this was not a fruitful thought. Amalgamation of the two cancer charities has been brought about since commencing writing this book.

The Campaign moved from premises in Grosvenor Place near Hyde Park Corner to a splendid building in Carlton House Terrace – Number 10 – financed for us by the Sobel family. We shared it with the Royal College of Pathologists.

Parallel with the Executive Committee was the Scientific Committee consisting of a large number of distinguished doctors and scientists presided over through most of my time by Sir Theo Crawford, a delightful man. When I was first Chairman their main task was to vet applications for grants for research. These were confined to costs of the research and direct expenses relating to it. We did not finance premises or other facilities. This changed when lack of funding by Government resulted in universities and other institutions not being able to accommodate research. Therefore we were compelled to provide some money for ancillary facilities including premises from time to time. My own thought at the time was that the Committee should be more proactive in the lines of research it should follow.

It now seems remarkable that in 1970 there was no department of medicine designated as concerned with cancer nor was there any career structure in that field. It seemed to me that a career structure should be created and that the start should be the endowment and creation of Chairs in Oncology, of which there were then none. This was done and is now widespread. Each Chair was endowed with about £500,000 to cover the incumbent, assistance and support.

Of course appeals had to be made and we had an Appeals Committee and its own secretariat. It was unnecessary to explain why support was necessary, but stimulating giving and organising appeals was essential. In 1970 I believe total receipts were about two million pounds per annum. They are now around sixty million per annum. The total amount available from voluntary sources has been greater than that provided by Government.

Locally around Collyers I made appeals at various functions, particularly dress shows put on by a local boutique with their own 'models' who were home-grown. We had a very good show at Bignor Park by kind permission of Lord Mersey and in Bosham and elsewhere. It was great fun and we raised quite a lot of money.

On one occasion I sailed to Alderney to present a prize to the Committee for raising so much money. On that occasion I had a member of the crew I did not know well. He went missing and, with the Chairman of the Appeal Committee, I went round the pubs – Alderney has more per square mile than any other place – but to no avail. Eventually I returned to the boat for the night where he turned up in the early morning, having been dead drunk in the bottom of another boat he had visited!

Fundraising was of course a central feature of the Campaign though this was not my main function. Nevertheless a number of fundraising functions were held each year which of course I attended. The most interesting one was a picnic at Windsor to which several hundred people came, some by horseback, from distant parts of the country picking up money on the way. In fact it was great fun and we had a lovely day, but we made very little money in relation to the effort made because of the expense of laying it on.

There was a campaigning organisation called ASH devoted to stopping smoking. At the time I was a heavy smoker. The Secretary of the CRC was David Gribben, a retired Brigadier and very efficient. As with most secretaries of organisations in my experience, he was inclined to drive the organisation forward and it was extremely difficult to control him! He was very keen to have a close relationship with ASH and to pursue their propaganda with them. I was against this partly because it would have been hypocritical of me as a smoker and partly because I did not think it right for the CRC to be a pressure group. Also he wanted the CRC to be involved in cancer education which again I thought a mistake. My concern was that we should stick to research into the causes and cure of cancer and that any dilution of this would be a mistake and possibly reduce public support. I lost this battle!

In time the CRC required more space in the building and the only source was to take some from the pathologists, whom Sir Theo knew well, so I asked him to approach them. He went to see the Secretary and was successful. Indeed they got on so well that having lost his first wife, he married her. I was thus instrumental in engineering connubial bliss as well as chairing the Campaign!

I had for some time been a Member of the Council of The Royal Society of Arts and in 1973 received a letter written on behalf of the President, Prince Philip, saying that he was forming a Working Group consisting of the RSA, the Committee for Environmental Conservation and the Institute of Fuel to report on 'Energy and the Environment'. At that time this was a novel idea and the letter said that as the writer knew of no one who knew less about either the environment or energy than I, would I be Chairman? Who could refuse such an invitation?

The members of the Working Party included Dr Chesters and Dr Fells of the Institute of Fuel, Keith Grant who was Secretary of the RSA and Robin Grove White of CPRE, all of whom became friends for long after this enquiry. There were also others who attended meetings including Aubrey Jones who had been a Minister in Government and Schumacher who had made his name with his book *Small is Beautiful,* concerned with intermediate technology for use in the developing countries. It was a very interesting experience in an entirely new field.

We had no secretariat and so each member wrote the part in his particular field of knowledge and I wrote the Introduction. Our main recommendation was the creation of a permanent Standing Commission on Energy and the Environment to integrate the development of energy policy and social environmental policy. It was a matter of pride for me that, when the Commission was formed many years

1983 Royal Commission on Environmental Pollution
Merton College, Oxford.
Thornton, Clark, Larminie, the author, Radice,
Schultz, Cummings, Acheson, Williams, Fogg, Cranbrook, Dore, Wilkinson,
Suckling, Warnock, Southwood, Clayton, Archer.

later and published its first and – as it turned out – its only Report under Lord Flowers on Coal and the Environment, the first paragraph quoted with approval that Report. 'Lord Nathan wrote, "A policy for the development of energy resources must be created in the context of its environmental and social consequences ... Protection of the environment cannot be separated from the other objects of a policy for energy, the present skirmishing between environmental interests and the energy industries benefits neither side".'

I did not at the time realise that this was a new concept which was then adopted. I believe it was partly this that resulted later in my being invited to join the Royal Commission on Environmental Pollution. Lord Flowers was a very distinguished nuclear physicist who chaired the Royal Commission on Environmental Pollution when studying nuclear waste and produced a memorable Report, became Rector of Imperial College, later Vice Chancellor of London University and then Chancellor of Manchester University. Approval by him was exciting. The Commission was 'put into abeyance' immediately after publication of the monumental Report on Coal and the Environment; i.e. killed! Mrs Thatcher did not like independent commissions because they were outside her control, and she preferred to exercise control over publication of advice which she could do if the Reports were made within the Civil Service machine.

It happened that shortly after receiving this invitation to Chair the Working Party the oil crisis broke; shortages of oil were imminent and the price went through the roof, so this seemed a particularly important and relevant assignment – and urgent. We set to work in the autumn of 1973 and published in mid-1974, which for that sort of job was rather quick.

In this Report we referred to nuclear power and the excellence of the safety record, but pointed to the possibility of trouble as less conscientious staff manned the plants after the passage of time. At a meeting of the Council of the RSA I was attacked for this by the head of the Atomic Energy Authority (who was very friendly and whom I greatly liked), but I told him it was my report not his. I think it may partly be due to this that shortly afterwards I was invited to be Chairman of the RSA.

The Chairman of the RSA holds office for two years and one of his first duties it to give the Inaugural Lecture. I chose 'Is Charity Redundant?' as my title largely because I had long been interested in charities and partly because I was in the middle of writing a Report on Charities and Voluntary Bodies.

This came about because Lord Goodman had been asked by the NCVO (National Council for Voluntary Organisations) to chair a committee to report on Charity because of articles in the press, said to be by the Charity Law Reform Society, which the NCVO wished to counter. In fact the Society so far as I know consisted of one person who decided he would get much more publicity if he called himself a 'Society'. This I find is quite common! I was asked to be Vice Chairman which was quite onerous as Lord Goodman was too busy to attend much. The Report was divided into sections of which the first, which I wrote, was concerned with the scope of charity and other parts with administration. Incidentally Lord Goodman was a man of large dimensions and Chandler came to fetch us one day in the office car. We both got in the back and Chandler said, 'Gentlemen, we cannot do this again. I cannot see over the bonnet'!

Whilst writing this Inaugural Lecture took less time than others I had to do, it was nevertheless a major operation. I showed it to Philippa's father JB who said it ought to qualify for a Doctorate which I took as a kind joke. When some time later Sussex University conferred an Honorary Doctorate on me this lecture was quoted!

As Chairman I had to visit many places to speak about the RSA and what it does, sometimes on subjects in which the Society was active, but of which I was largely ignorant, such as design. I had to give such a talk at Bangor. Philippa and I went there and were put up in the students' hostel which was sparsely furnished with a bed which was so small I could not get into it. I slept on the floor! On this visit we went on to Lord Aberconway's marvellous garden which I had visited earlier with the Gardeners.

The Franklin Room in the Society's House needed redecoration and an American Fellow decided to give us the money for this. We had a great party there to thank him and to put up a plaque to commemorate his generosity. He seems to have been so overwhelmed by this that he said he would arrange for me to become an Honorary Sheriff of Dallas, his home city. In due course I received a Certificate and badge – and only lacked the six-shooter.

1976 was the Bicentennial of the USA and as Benjamin Franklin was very active in the Society in its earliest days I was invited by Philadelphia to give the Bicentennial Address at the Franklin Institute there. Preparation was a formidable task and I was grateful for the enormous help given me by Mr Allen, the Society's archivist. That was a particularly hard time as my second year in office was about to commence and I had been challenged by Maisie Webb, a Member of the Council and formerly of the Patent Office, to give my second Inaugural Lecture on Patents – and I had accepted the challenge. I suppose preparation of that lecture took three months and forty or so hours, so I was fairly exhausted.

The Hall in Philadelphia was formidably large; it must have held around two hundred people and was packed. In the middle was a forty-foot statue of the great man whom I thus addressed! This was a full dress lecture and of some length and as it gives some history of the Society I append a copy (Appendix I). Keith Grant was Secretary of the Society and a delightful man whose wife had been a prima ballerina. When we were in New York later we went to a café frequented by artists and there was her picture permanently hung on the wall.

We made a number of other visits while in the States including attending and speaking to the English Speaking Union in Washington where the average age must have been a hundred! We went on to New Brunswick, Canada and there I had to speak to a Chapter of the Society in a restaurant. Speaking in a room with other diners is not easy. We had I suppose forty people present. I described what the Society was doing, but either from boredom or over-excitement at my remarks, one of our number fainted and so this brought the proceedings to an end!

Prince Philip was President of the Society and very interested and active. He read the minutes of the Council meetings and one soon knew if he disapproved of decisions! From 1970 he used the Society as a main platform for his environmental interests and often had meetings at Buckingham Palace which I attended. He was extremely knowledgeable on all matters environmental and one had to be very well-informed when meeting him on such a subject. Once he had made up his mind on something it was extremely difficult to get him to change it. I had a great admiration for his knowledge and grasp of many subjects.

When the President of the Royal Academy died Prince Philip asked me to represent him at the funeral at St Margaret's, Piccadilly. This meant dressing up in a morning coat and I arrived thus at Buckingham Palace – but without a top hat as required. There is a 'Palace top hat' available for all and since it is not worn, size does not matter. The Royal Daimler (without number plates) was provided for my use in which I arrived at the church where I sat in the front pew and was treated as if it was he, not me! After this I returned to Buckingham Palace and left the hat there. By an extraordinary chance

I met there Rupert's House Master at Charterhouse who was keeper of the Queen's stamps, so my stock went up with him!

There were lighter sides to life at the Society. Each year we had a soirée when some leading musician would give a recital and we would then have a good buffet supper in the rooms available. It was there that I first heard – and met – Felicity Lot in her earlier days before she had become so famous. On another occasion we had a famous pianist to give us a recital and I went to meet him immediately before he was to enter the Great Room. He was in a terrible state of nerves – and no wonder as earlier in the day he had come to try out the piano and the acoustics, and two of the keys got stuck. He had sent for Steinway – the piano makers – who had come and were supposed to have put it right and he had satisfied himself they had, but was nervous the trouble might recur. Fortunately it did not and we had a magnificent performance. But it always has seemed to me perilous to play an unknown piano and not one's own instrument as a violinist does.

These soirées were smart occasions and I had the privilege on one occasion of sitting next to the viola player of the Amadeus Quartet who was a delightful and modest man. I always regarded that Quartet as the world number one for Mozart.

In earlier times the soirée had been rather formal and I remember my father taking me to one at the beginning of the war when dress was white tie and tails, and I saw one of the Hapsburg family there with the famous lip!

In time Keith retired as Secretary to do other things and Christopher Lucas was appointed in his place. He was quite a different sort of person to Keith having been concerned in administration far more extensively. Shortly after his appointment he was approached about the launch of a book in the Society's house and, after full consultation with others who had been with the Society for many years, agreed. We had quite often launches of books from the House. It was however a grave embarrassment to him when the day after the launch the Society's name appeared for the first time on page three of *The Sun*. This was the page of the naked ladies! At a Council meeting held shortly afterwards he told members about this with great embarrassment and most of those present looked quite blank. So I went round the table to ask the twenty or so members of the Council – all very distinguished citizens – which of them knew about page three. Only one admitted to it!

Life was always busy at the Society because our main purpose was to initiate new ideas, or to bring together those who had worked separately on related matters with a view to stimulating new approaches and then passing on to others the work involved in exploiting them. Following lectures I introduced seminars from time to time to bring together those involved to get the arrangements going. It was interesting but time-consuming.

In 1979 Sir Hans Kornberg, then Chairman of the Royal Commission on Environmental Pollution, invited me to lunch and to become a member of it. This was a high honour as every word the Commission uttered was treated with enormous respect, so I accepted with pleasure.

The Royal Commission reports to the Queen, not to Government, a privilege which we jealously guarded, as it prevented our being influenced or interfered with by Government. Our opinions were our own. Members were appointed by the Queen on the advice of the Prime Minister and generally remained for around three years. I was there for ten. There were about sixteen members of whom around twelve were scientists and the rest non-scientists – sometimes a philosopher (Mary Warnock) or an economist (Emma Rothschild), a business man (John Raisman) or a Trade Unionist (John Edmunds), or a lawyer (David Williams). I was rather an oddball as I was not appointed as a lawyer, although I was naturally asked from time to time about legal matters, but primarily because of the RSA Report on Energy and the Environment. We had a staff of three plus secretarial assistance so it was a small office. There was a Secretary, a Scientific Secretary and one other. When I went to the USA and met the Environmental Protection Agency (who did quite a different job) they were complaining that their staff had been reduced to twelve thousand and they were amazed at our arrangements – and that all members were unpaid!

Most of the members were academics and of course received their pay as such and the universities on the whole thought membership was good for them. It was the most delightful group of people I had

The author at The Royal Society of Arts in front of the roll of past Chairmen following the first environmental lecture in his name.

ever had the privilege of working with. You could ask any question on any subject without embarrassment and always got a good answer; nobody pressed himself forward for the sake of impressing others as so often happens. I made many lasting friendships there. Being a scientific layman one of the scientists who had drafted out something would fix me with a steely gaze and say, 'And what does the man on the Clapham omnibus think about that?' and I would reply that I could not understand a word of it, and they would redraft! Such was our relationship with one another. The first Report with which I was involved was on Marine Oil Pollution. Our reports were long and thorough and took around two years to produce. Most of the writing was by the Secretary and the Scientific Secretary with participation by Members who had special knowledge or interest in certain sections. On this Report we had as Members an environmental officer from British Petroleum (who was a permanent Member like all the rest) and Lady (Irene) White who was Chairman of ACOPS (Advisory Committee on Pollution of the Sea). Lady White was at the time Chairman of the House of Lords Select Committee on the European Communities and it was she who in due course invited me to join that Committee and its sub-committee on the Environment.

Members were supplied with a full-sized four-drawer filing cabinet delivered to home and a Gladstone bag for carrying the papers, adorned with the Royal Crest. On termination of membership the filing cabinet was generally removed, but in my case I think I had been a Member so long they forgot!

We took a great deal of evidence, mostly written, and one Report would require the whole filing cabinet for space for evidence, so there was a lot of reading to be done. With experience this came quicker, but was nevertheless a great burden. We then selected whom we would see and take evidence orally. Taking evidence was really a discussion with the witness and very informal. There was never any lack of witnesses who wished to give us evidence. These Reports were an educational exercise for all of us as we had no knowledge – or detailed knowledge – of the wide variety of subjects covered.

This enquiry into Marine Oil Pollution involved geology and natural seepage of oil, construction of ships and the impact on the environment of accidents and how ships might be designed to avoid accidents, identification of sources of oil by chemical analysis, clearing up oil spills and the impact of chemicals used on the marine environment, marking of hazards at sea and the impact on wildlife of oil pollution and resultant death of great populations of birds and fish and other wild life. There was also the change in the ecology on the seabed resulting from exploiting oil resources. These are just a few of the matters which spring to mind.

One bad accident off the Brittany coast resulted in a huge oil spill and thousands of birds died. Our marine biologist pointed out that these birds were at the extremity of their habitat and there was no question of the species being in danger of extinction. From that point of view he was quite relaxed. The oil polluted and clung to rocks for a great stretch of the North Brittany coast and questions arose as to the least damaging means of cleaning up. There was much concern about the responsibility of the owners and the captain of the ship, between whom there seemed to be some confusion. Of course it was not for us to adjudicate or answer any of these questions, but as the accident occurred during our study, it was helpful for us to have such experience before us. We were invited to France to discuss matters with the French Minister and the Naval people at Brest. We were accompanied to these meetings by a member of the British Embassy.

At Brest we were entertained to lunch at a feast after which we were led into a room for a lecture with illustrations about this accident. Our Embassy representative had been overcome by the feast and was fast asleep and our French host said he thought we had lost him. We had! Hans Kornberg and I were in similar condition and only remained awake by feigning short sight and getting up to look closely at each illustration! It was on this expedition that I got permission to moor my yacht in the summer in the naval port of Brest to start on a cruise of Western and Southern Brittany.

During this study we also had to go to the Forties Field in the North Sea to a platform to see how this worked. We travelled up to Aberdeen and donned survival suits (of which I had ordered one to fit, being so large) and got into a large helicopter and flew out low over the sea in thick fog to the platform which we circled and then landed with great skill on the tiny platform. We learnt that fish were plentiful beneath and around the platform due to the heat of the water, but that fishing was prohibited due to the risk of catching a diver! The restaurant and food were excellent to maintain morale and the term for remaining there quite long. Sensibly, in my view, women were excluded from being on board. We learnt a lot about the extraction of the oil from the seabed and its storage and shipment ashore by ship or pipeline and the dangers of each. It was a fascinating and most informative visit. It was brought to an early close as one of the crew of a neighbouring platform had been taken ill and needed urgently to be taken to hospital ashore. We got into our helicopter and went off in thick fog to the other platform where we landed being unable to see the landing pad (I hoped the pilot could!), picked the patient up and returned to Aberdeen.

One of the great pleasures of these studies was that about four months before completion we went to the College of the Chairman (during my time, either at Oxford or Cambridge) and stayed for three or four days to thrash out the really difficult questions which had to be resolved. This was the most interesting experience as we were all totally uninhibited and we had really wide-ranging discussions in a very relaxed atmosphere. I remember that following the waste enquiry under Dick Southwood we went to his College – Merton, notable for its hospitality – and saying to him that it was fortunate that we had serious discussions on the subject of our Report to fill the time between meals!

Our study of waste sounds dull, though I became really interested in it; but it was during this time that my sight deteriorated so much that I had difficulty in reading the papers. However Dick was very supportive and we produced a pretty good Report, most of the recommendations of which were later incorporated into legislation; the Bill came before the House of Lords and I was able to put forward a lot of amendments based on this Report almost all of which were accepted.

During this study we visited the Midlands and certain waste facilities there. One of these was a site for disposal of waste oil for cleaning and re-use. One of the rules was that oil incorporating poly chlorinated biphenols (PCBs) had to be disposed of to special waste facilities due to its adverse chemical effects. I felt by instinct that the boss of this waste facility might well be receiving oil contaminated with PCBs and mixing it with ordinary waste oil and might be taking money for doing so. It cost quite a lot to dispose of oil polluted with PCBs and when I sat next to him at dinner my fears were increased. I told Dick Southwood of my thoughts. It was therefore with some satisfaction that I read in the press some time later that he had been convicted of this offence and I think sent to prison.

On a jollier note, one of the visits – for a purpose I cannot remember – was to Selwyn College, Cambridge where we were put up in their new hostel building. Gathorne Cranbrook was in the next room to mine. At about 2 a.m. I heard some stones being thrown at my window and so I put on my dressing gown to see what was up and looked out to find a girl student in distress clearly wanting to come into the building. So I told her to wait in what I thought was a whisper. However it woke Gathorne who appeared in my room concerned that I was ill. I told him the problem and we went downstairs together and found doors and windows locked. So we opened Barbara Clayton's (Professor Dame Barbara Clayton, formerly President of the Royal Society of Pathologists) door and found there was a little kitchen and sink off the corridor there and that her room was beyond. The kitchen window was open so we called the girl and heaved her in over the sink and she ran off very frightened! I was concerned that this might get into the press as 'Members of the Royal Commission and their night-time frolics with girl students', but fortunately it never got out. Incidentally after I had the cardiac arrest and was feeling miserable it was Barbara who told me that was entirely normal and I would be all right after a year. Nobody else had told me and it cheered me greatly that it would come to an end!

It was at Selwyn College that a conference was held, which I was asked to Chair, on Water Privatisation. A don called Guruswarmy from Sri Lanka, who used to send me his papers on the environment for comment, I think organised it. Government had in mind privatisation and there was much difference of opinion as to its desirability. The Conference was firmly against this and I agreed! The idea was dropped and it was much later that it was revived and implemented.

Following this Report on waste I came in touch with the newly formed Institute of Wastes Management where I was asked to speak from time to time and invited for a number of years to their annual conference in Torquay – to speak. They held it in Torquay as there was a large area outside where machines could be exhibited including vast 'Vultures' for collecting waste. They made me an Honorary Fellow by which I was much honoured and I am still invited to an annual meeting to discuss matters. I made quite a lot of friends there.

Lead was a subject causing widespread concern partly because of a report that lead in petrol was resulting in harm to children. We embarked on a study of lead and divided it into two – one in petrol and one in other contexts such as paint. We did not agree about the effect on children (under review by our medical and scientific Members including particularly Barbara Clayton), but we thought the concentration was far higher than was safe and far higher than other substances, so we recommended it be removed from petrol. I advised that this must be a matter for EC legislation rather than purely UK, a view with which at first Government did not agree, but eventually they did and the UK took the lead in abolition of lead in petrol throughout the EC.

At the end of our study we were asked to address Ministers and others on the subject which of course we agreed to. There were three of us – Dick Southwood, the Member from BP and myself. I found it very satisfactory that the large number of Ministers – and a Secretary of State – should be sitting at desks before us and we should be teaching them. Within two days Government announced its decision to adopt our recommendations. It was certainly the quickest response to one of our Reports we had ever had.

Of the other Reports we did perhaps the Report on Genetically Modified Organisms was the most interesting. I was very keen we should do this urgently as I was fearful that in the absence of public confidence in the controls on escape to the environment, a similar situation of frustration as had occurred with nuclear power would arise. I felt that genetic engineering had a tremendous amount to offer and such frustration leading to a block on development would be very damaging, so I urged that we should carry out the study which we did. There were questions relating to patents and the reactions of the chemical industry to the very strict controls we had in mind. I went to see ICI on two or three occasions and found that it was unnecessary to emphasise the necessity for strict controls to avoid adverse public opinion; they recognised that it was adverse public reaction to development of GMOs that was the greatest danger. The Advisory Committee on Releases to the Environment (ACRE) was to be the central point for decision as to what might be done. So strict were we in our recommendations that we said no categories of release should be permitted and each release must be considered separately; only with much experience should categories of release be permitted.

After publication a number of chemical companies complained that the regulations suggested were much too strict and far stricter than in the USA and that this would adversely effect competition. However for a long time there was no adverse comment by environmental interests – including Friends of the Earth and Greenpeace – and we seem to have got it right. It was after the BSE crisis and its adverse effect on the opinion of scientists that opposition to releases of GMOs developed, and the irresponsible actions of Greenpeace in invading farmland were supported by much public opinion. It struck me as odd that the Minister of Science, when confronted with this, never referred to his own ACRE as the body created years previously to deal with these problems, and I told him so, to no effect. Indeed I phoned the Secretary of ACRE and spoke to the Chairman – Professor Beringer – suggesting they should publicise their existence and responsibilities, but to no avail.

After ten years' membership I decided in 1989 I should retire from the Commission. One tends to get stale after writing many Reports and I thought it was best for the Commission to find fresh minds.

It was around this time that I was asked to chair a new organisation – the Institute of Environmental Assessment – which was in the process of being formed. Environmental Assessment is a process required in relation to large development projects and there was some EC law as well as UK law on it. It is related to the planning process and I knew little about it. I agreed to be Chairman for a year to start it off. One of its objects was to improve and standardise the product and this was desired by many of the local authorities, the Department of Environment and their Inspectors. There were two professors who were helpful and I came to know Professor Christopher Wood quite well. Indeed I got him to help us on this subject when

I was Chairman of the National Grid Environmental Advisory Panel. There were those on the Committee who wanted to extend its activities, with which I did not agree. Major planning enquiries such as that required for nuclear power projects required extensive Assessments and the main one of these at the time related to the nuclear project in Suffolk, which eventually was built, the Inspector being the leading expert in the field, Sir Frank Layfield. When my year came to an end I persuaded him to take over the Chairmanship, under whom they were much better served than under me!

I had had to retire from Senior Partnership of the firm and I decided as my sight returned that it would be sensible and safer to embark on fresh fields of law rather than continue with what I had been doing. This was because, having been out of touch with developments for some two years, I thought I would always be in danger of acting on the law as it had been without regard to developments in my absence. Law, particularly on tax, changes fast. Having done a lot in the environmental field I thought this would be an interesting one to explore albeit at that time there was no recognised 'environmental law'. This idea was enhanced by the break up of HON & V and my transfer in early 1989 with many other Partners to Denton Hall where John Salter was the Partner in charge of Property and particularly wanted me to help develop the environmental field.

In all, 1988 had been a bad year! Obviously the break-up of the old family firm hit one hard. Philippa lost her hearing that year during the trip to New Zealand. Perhaps it was not surprising that my health suffered; I was diagnosed as having a clot in my leg and had to go into King Edward VII Hospital, Midhurst where I also had severe pains all over as if I had arthritis in every joint. Shortly after that I had to have a pacemaker fitted.

However, it had been a matter of immense satisfaction to me that shortly before all this, Sussex University had expressed the wish to confer on me the Honorary Degree of Doctor of Laws and the ceremony was to be held at a time when I was still in hospital. I was determined to go – and I did, using a stick. For me it really was a great occasion and Beno ter Keile from our EC Club in Holland came over for the occasion in his professor's gown as holder of a

1988 University of Sussex
The author with Lord Hailsham (Lord Chancellor), right, and Lord Emlyn Jones (former Lord Chancellor) after degrees of Honorary Doctor of Laws had been conferred.

chair at Utrecht. Lord Hailsham and Lord Emlyn Jones – both Lord Chancellors present or past – were the others so honoured, so I was in good company. I was very pleased with the citation read out on the occasion which I append (Appendix II).

It was in the early 1990s that Philippa and I received an invitation from the Duke of Richmond to dine with him at Goodwood to meet the new Vice Chancellor of Sussex University, Leslie Fielding, who seemed a nice enough person. I understood he had been a senior figure in the diplomatic service, had been our Ambassador in Iran and had learnt Persian in three weeks! After he was appointed I was asked to join the Council of the University, and whilst some of the discussions were interesting, I had little to do. However I became increasingly concerned that students were dropping out because they were unable to afford the cost of being there, which was wasting money and talent and was very bad for the morale of the students affected. Students seemed to come without regard to the financial cost – particularly perhaps those who were married. My own thought was that perhaps some form of means-testing should be applied to avoid this, but this was not politically acceptable. There was a small fund provided by Government to meet cases of hardship but it was so small it would have been sufficient to provide ten pounds to each student in need. No progress was made!

After about five years Leslie had to retire due to his wife's health. The position of Vice Chancellor had to be filled and a Committee was formed of which I was a member. There were eight of us including Chairman of Council and the Treasurer, about five members of faculties and myself. We had many applications, but during the sittings of the Committee, Gordon Conway (whom I had met on the Royal Commission and came to know quite well) wrote to me saying he was going to apply. He had no idea I was on the Committee. I told him of this and reported fully to the Committee. The Chairman very much wanted to appoint a Civil Servant who would know his way round Whitehall and one of the applicants was the Permanent Secretary at the Home Office. Eventually the choice was between these two and interviews were held, from which I got the impression that the Permanent Secretary neither knew about nor was interested in Education. Eventually there was a vote on the Committee which I called, and strongly supported Gordon whom all the Members knew I had known over the years and admired. Gordon won and the Chairman and the Treasurer were defeated. I do not believe the Chairman ever forgave me and indeed retired not long after Gordon took up office.

I served on various Committees of the University and was in close touch with Gordon who invited me to various affairs at the University, including some at his home which was provided by the University at Swanborough Manor, which by a curious coincidence had been given by Stella Reading to the University on her death. Gordon and his wife Sue (who is expert on Thai design and teaches) loved it there and planted an orchard of old-fashioned apple trees with great success. After about five years there, Gordon was invited to become President of the Rockefeller Foundation in New York and the University released him to take this up. He was succeeded by Alasdair Smith, a professor at the University who had been a member of the Committee which appointed Gordon. He wanted to live at his own home so Swanborough Manor ceased to be the Vice Chancellor's home.

After a total of nine years on the Council I retired. Increasingly I found myself asked to lecture on environmental matters at this time and as a result really became part of what I call the environmental mafia! I lectured at various commercially organised seminars or took the chair at them and in time was asked to be President of the NSCA (National Society for Clean Air), the oldest environmental organisation in this country, having been formed in 1899 to combat smoke pollution. This was a great honour. Most of the members came from local authorities but some were from industry. Those attending included a number of environmental health officers of whose Institute I had become Vice President. They had originated as sanitary inspectors, but their responsibilities increased to cover an enormous range of matters including restaurants, air pollution, noise and other nuisances. The quality of officers had improved enormously and I took the opportunity of mentioning this in the House when appropriate. I met many of them and other officers of local authorities at annual gatherings and much enjoyed this.

The increase in concern at pollution had extended so far beyond air pollution in recent years that the functions of the NSCA had likewise to be broadened and in consequence the question of some change in name arose. After dinner and over wine I discussed this with the Secretary and eventually came up with 'The Society for Clean Living' which I immediately withdrew as we would not have any qualified members! Eventually it was changed to The Society for Clean Air and Environmental Protection, which I find too long and boring!

In 1987 Richard Macrory had approached me when he and others had in mind to form a UK Environmental Law Association and asked me to be President. I readily agreed. The first members were mostly young academic lawyers. Richard (now a professor who has held a Chair at Imperial College, had a spell at Oxford and is now at UCL) became a member of the Royal Commission and was far more orientated towards legal matters than I ever was there. Another member was Stephen Tromans, then at Selwyn College Cambridge, who later joined a Cambridge firm of solicitors and then headed the Environment Department (which he largely formed) at Simmons & Simmons, eventually going to the Bar. Incidentally, when I was Chairman of the House of Lords Environment Sub-committee, each of them helped me as specialist adviser.

At an early meeting of UKELA a lot of lawyers there objected to the formation of such an association on the ground that there was no such thing as 'environmental law'. That was in 1987. We had originally about fifty members and within a year or so two to three thousand. It became the fastest-growing branch of legal practice.

We instituted an annual lecture we called the Garner Lecture named after a professor in Nottingham who had played a leading part in the development of this branch of law, and who had now become blind. He always came – sometimes with his friend at Nottingham, Professor John Smith, who was my specialist adviser in the Murder Report. Richard asked me to give the first lecture and I worked hard at it and append a copy (Appendix III).

After one function Richard had arranged for us all to go to a pub for a drink and on this occasion we were in the open – there was no room inside – in the pouring rain. This was one reason why after each Garner Lecture when we had an audience of over a hundred I always arranged for a small party of the lecturer and Committee to be held at a good place – sometimes a restaurant, Athenaeum or QEII Conference Centre. It was at one of these Garner Lectures – given by Lord Woolf – that he first put forward the idea of an Environmental Court which he has since tried to flesh out.

In 1992 after five years I decided to retire as President and secured Gordon Slynn (Lord Slynn), a Law Lord, to succeed me. It was around this time that the positions of Lord Chief Justice and Master of the Rolls became vacant and had to be filled. There was an idea that two of our leading judges – Peter Taylor and Harry Woolf – should be appointed. I thought it a bad idea to appoint two Jewish judges to the most senior positions in the judiciary. In the event Peter Taylor was appointed LCJ and Harry a Law Lord. Peter Taylor was a remarkable man as a lawyer, played rugby for Northumberland and was a talented pianist. He gave a recital at Lincoln's Inn Hall and accompanied others on an occasion when I was there. It was only afterwards when I got home that I learnt that it had been announced on the radio that he was to retire due to cancer. To have given that recital in those circumstances seemed to me to show remarkable courage.

I received a very unexpected invitation at the instance of David Williams, who was then the first 'permanent' Vice Chancellor of Cambridge to be Chairman of the Home Office Animal Procedures Committee. This was created under the Animal Procedures Act and designed to reconcile the needs of animal welfare and medical research – clearly not wholly reconcilable! I was not enthusiastic to take this on, but because David Williams had suggested it I did.

The Committee had about twenty members representing animal welfare organisations, industry, vets, science and medicine as well as a philosopher and one or two other laymen. I found a remarkable unanimity of approach to the problems arising which was cheering, though there were naturally differences in emphasis.

As I had no knowledge of the subject, I decided to go to various laboratories and animal centres such as the apes centre near Small Dole, and found them all very disagreeable although I was told and could see that they were well run. The Committee considered applications for licences to carry out experiments on animals, which were first examined by civil servant scientists, whose recommendations were then considered in accordance with guidelines laid down by the Committee. For instance experiments involving primates were very strictly limited and rarely authorised, whilst numbers of animals involved were carefully examined. Animals involved in cosmetics production was a matter of wide public interest and I arranged for an extensive study of this to be made. All new products had as a matter of law to be animal-tested and often involved the use of many animals. However the tests related almost exclusively to skin troubles and in practically all cases produced no adverse results. The animals were mostly mice and they had their fur shaved, but otherwise did not suffer any consequence. If they did (which was rare) the person responsible was often sacked.

I received an invitation to chair a discussion on the work of the Committee on 'Newsnight' at which there would be one representative of animal welfare interests and another from pharmaceutical organisations. We met briefly prior to the programme; both were going to produce reasoned arguments and it looked as if it would be a good discussion. When we went into the studio I saw we were to sit at a concave table with a wall behind, on which were painted in the most lurid colours a cat and a dog with their entrails hanging out and in the utmost pain. My first reaction was to walk out. And then I thought perhaps I could with my considerable bulk obscure the whole picture, which I did! I regret that this is too typical of distortion of sensible discussion by irresponsible producers. My colleagues had the reasoned discussion we had envisaged. Next morning the police came to Collyers to warn me to check for explosives under my car regularly in view of the programme. Such was the atmosphere of fear and threat at the time.

Then the question of bringing cephalopods such as octopus within the scope of the Committee and the Act was raised, and much discussion on their reaction to procedures which in others might cause pain. It seemed to me a futile enquiry as there were hardly any experiments carried out upon them in this country or elsewhere. Further the real worry for the public had originally been in relation to primates, dogs and cats with some further concern for mice. Therefore as a matter of public relations I thought extension of the range of creatures protected would diminish the impact on the public of what we were doing. However, I lost this argument! I decided after three years I would retire. Since then it has struck me as extraordinary that Government has never mentioned this committee and its work in the context of animal welfare campaigns particularly after the violent onslaught on Huntingdon Laboratories. It might be thought that the animal rights activists were the first to think of animal welfare!

David Williams asked me subsequently to chair the Disciplinary Court of Cambridge University. This had been held for some five years by a Lord Justice of Appeal and nothing had happened, but the vacancy had to be filled and carried membership of the University. I accepted as an honour.

In the first year there were three rather sad cases of cheating induced by excessive pressure by over-ambitious parents. I sat with four members of Faculties (not legal) and quite a good secretariat provided by the University. We tried to find a suitable penalty, not too severe but sufficient to show our disapproval – and I hope we succeeded. Far different was a case in my third year of a mature student in his thirties, an American, who said he had very advanced qualifications in medicine and who came to Cambridge to take History of Art. He was at Trinity. He was accused by the University of a sophisticated cheating programme and appeared with solicitors and Counsel in what turned out to be a full two-day hearing. It struck me as strange that his tutor was not there as tutors normally support their students in all circumstances. I was shocked also that a reference from the USA was passed by him to us and had not been sent direct to the University or his solicitors. These were merely incidents in a case which we found proved against him and my recommendation, with which the members of faculty sitting with me agreed, was that he should be expelled from the University. He decided to appeal to the *septem viri* as he was entitled to do. I phoned Sir Andrew Huxley who had long since retired as Master of Trinity (and whom I knew as a Governor of Priors Field School where Jenny and Nicola had been and a member of the Animal Procedures Committee) as to who these were and he told me they were Heads of Houses. I said I supposed it was a very ancient body and he confirmed it was. However, they had been six members with a Chairman until before the first War when JBS Haldane was summoned to appear. That was just after the accepted pronunciation of the letter 'v' in Latin had been altered from 'v' to 'w'. The result was that the Committee came to be known as 'sexweery' which was thought not to be appropriate! So they changed the Committee from six plus a Chairman to seven and thus became *septem viri*! After three years I retired bearing in mind that I was then almost seventy.

Around 1990 I was approached by David Jefferies, Chairman of the newly privatised National Grid Company, to join the Environment Development Advisory Panel to be chaired by John Horlock. I agreed. John Horlock was a distinguished engineer.

Under John's guidance we looked at tower design and the set-up for monitoring environmental performance which was the responsibility of the environment manager Stephen Hill. He came from the CEGB, was knowledgeable about environmental matters and knew most of the people in the field. John also became interested in various reports about the health risks arising from high-voltage transmission lines due to electric and magnetic discharges. The suggestion had been made that leukaemia in children arose from this source and particularly from connections near their bedrooms. This of course raised serious matters for us. He called in Professor Doll who was a leading epidemiologist (and had found the connection between smoking and cancer) who reported that the fears were unfounded. However public concern continued to rise with reports both from Scandinavia and the USA and was taken up by the press. My own view was that we were not equipped to deal with this either by the knowledge of the membership of the Panel (which contained no medics) or our terms of reference. In time concern slackened and we ceased to devote attention to it.

John retired as Chairman and became Treasurer of the Royal Society which is a whole-time job and I took over the Chairmanship. There was much pressure to require the Company to put its lines underground and thus eliminate the visual pollution arising from the towers and lines striding across the countryside. The objection to doing so which had been adopted by the Company rested solely on cost – about twenty times the cost for 'undergrounding' as for towers and overhead lines. It seemed to me that this defence was unlikely to satisfy the public nor was I convinced that there was undiluted environmental benefit from doing so. I initiated a major enquiry into this and largely wrote the final Report myself. There were a lot of most interesting aspects to this enquiry.

First a trench the width of half a motorway (including the hard shoulder) was required to deal with the heat created by the transmission. Therefore there would be an enormous scar in the

1992: the author, Chairman of Sussex Downs Conservation Board with Hazen and Wispa at the signpost on Bignor Hill.
Reproduced by kind permission of the *West Sussex Gazette.*

countryside and severe hydrological questions in many sites. Second, the maintenance was far more complex and faults more frequent than with overhead transmission. Third, increased transmission capacity in existing lines overhead which had been developed to avoid the necessity of introducing more towers and lines could not be accepted by underground cables – partly because of increased heat generation. And of course there was the increased cost of undergrounding – around twenty times that of overhead cables.

We had evidence from ecological experts on the possibility of recovery of different soils from disturbance in laying underground cables which linked with experience I was having on quite a different scale and different circumstances at the Sussex Downs Conservation Board.

The need for such a published and widely read Report arose not only from general public interest, but also the need to persuade planning inspectors of the position, as they were frequently minded to require undergrounding as part of a consent to permit a line to be erected: and so such a report was published and I believe had some impact.

I was anxious that the staff of the company should not regard the Panel as enemies of the company as has frequently happened elsewhere in the context of environment and therefore proposed that we should make at least one visit per year to operating units to discuss these matters with them. I believe this had a favourable effect. It resulted in visits arranged by the company to excellent hotels all over the country which we greatly enjoyed. My job seemed to be to choose the menu and wines which I also enjoyed! It gave us the opportunity of seeing aspects of the operations in action such as stringing lines overhead in Snowdonia using helicopters; a completed new overhead line in Lincolnshire and the problems attendant on completing the job; various substations in the countryside and in London, and the central control complex near the office by Bankside Power Station and then in Wokingham. Visits to substations gave us the opportunity to meet senior project management teams who had little contact with executives of the company and discuss the relevance of environmental factors in their capital expenditure as well as the very important contaminated land programmes. We learnt a lot and I like to think they did too. I did feel we must meet at least once a year in Coventry, the company's HQ and we did, but otherwise (apart from meetings around the country) the meetings were in the London office.

One of the major troubles for the company related to planning consents for new lines required, often to link up new power stations – and some big ones were built after privatisation in the north-east. They necessitated not only lines to link them to the grid, but also some modification of the existing lines for reinforcement or otherwise. Local opposition was generally fierce as overhead lines spoilt the countryside and inspectors at the public enquiries rightly placed great weight on this. I therefore thought it was all the more important that the company should present its case in the best possible way and that they should pay special attention to the Environmental Assessments submitted. A study was made of this and I brought in my friend Professor Chris Wood who was most helpful. At the same time Sir John Burnett was working on the possibility of introducing computer imaging to supplement this. Generally I asked members of the Panel with special knowledge to lead the various enquiries and they were a remarkable group including Andrew Derbyshire, architect, Mrs Colwyn Foulkes, landscape architect and expert on National Parks, and John Burnett, biologist and former Principal of Edinburgh University.

I greatly enjoyed my time with the company but long before I actually retired I suggested I should because I thought they should have as Chairman someone with new ideas and who was younger. Eventually I retired in 2000 after some ten years on the Panel. Meantime in 1992 as I was about to be seventy, having retired from practice at Denton Hall and from practically all Committees and Trusts with which I had been involved, I was wondering how I was going to spend my time. I was delighted when visiting the Vice Chancellor's office at Sussex University to meet David Streeter who told me about the Sussex Downs Conservation Board and enquired whether I would be Chairman. I was very interested not least because I knew the Downs pretty well from hunting over the years.

The Board had been initiated by the Chief Planning Officers of East and West Sussex – Chris Williams and Peter Bryant – with a view to unifying policy of the thirteen local authorities in whose territory the AONB lay, and the Countryside Commission had been brought in to provide some finance and members of the Board. Julia Cumberledge (who was well known particularly in East Sussex County and Health circles) had been appointed Chairman; but shortly afterwards she had been appointed to Ministerial Office by the Government and had been made a Peer – hence the vacancy.

Chris Williams whom I had never met came to Collyers to inspect me and we had a long very friendly talk. This extended to the differences between East and West Sussex of which I then knew little as I had had nothing to do with local government. He pointed to the rural nature of West Sussex as compared with the large urban component in East Sussex (which then included Brighton and Hove). He said West Sussex was very feudal and I thought he was referring to the large landed estates such as Petworth, Cowdray and Norfolk. But he was not. He was speaking of the officers of the county whom he thought very feudal in their administration! At any rate I seemed to pass the test and was appointed.

Efforts had been made to appoint officers of the Board but these had not attracted candidates of appropriate calibre, so it was decided to start again. I was keen to appoint young people as this was a new venture and I thought the young were less likely to get into difficulties with the very experienced local authority officers with whom they would be dealing. We decided we needed three senior officers – a Sussex Downs Officer (CEO), a Countryside Officer and a Planning Officer.

As Sussex Downs Officer we chose Paul Tiplady who was in his early thirties and who said his ambition in life was to be National Parks Officer for Cumbria which was his home county. After about five years a vacancy arose for that position which he filled and left us. Martin Beaton who was in his mid-thirties was appointed as Countryside Officer and succeeded Paul. Simon Enderson who was in his late twenties was appointed Planning Officer and left us after about four years to become the youngest Planning Inspector in the country. So we did not select too badly!

We found an office at Storrington with Horsham District Council. It had six rooms but no room for expansion. This seemed to me essential as it is so easy to expand the office numbers – and this was impossible with the limited space. Having divided the AONB into areas we appointed area officers with staff of Rangers. The total staff was around twenty-nine, most of whom were Rangers working on the ground. The total size of the AONB was around 400 square miles and the population around 40,000. About one third of the AONB was in the Weald north of the Chalk Downs.

The first major problem we had related to the transfer of assets from local authorities to the Board, which was a complicated matter. So that it should not fester I asked Mr Kimmis, whom I had known at the Board of Trade companies department when I was in practice, to deal with this urgently which he did. Martin worked on the rights of way (which extended for over a thousand miles) to get information sorted out to introduce a work programme, all of which, after quite a short time, was computerised and available readily to Rangers as well as Area Managers and HQ. This was very successful.

There was a proposed by-pass of Worthing involving purchase by Government of housing along the intended road which was done long before the Board was formed. Then Government decided not to build a by-pass, so they sold all the houses they had bought. It was quite clear to me that a time would come when a by-pass had to be built and the route (following sale of all the houses) was bound to be through the Downs which was quite unacceptable to us. I wrote to the Secretary of the State to tell him this. In particular I pointed out that if the Government could not presently afford the by-pass it need not be built now, but the previously agreed route should be retained with the houses bought and the whole scheme put on ice. Their idea of giving up the scheme could only lead to future trouble. I got nowhere!

We had always felt that the Board should cover East Hampshire as well as Sussex, and with a view to getting co-operation with them we formed a joint committee under the chairmanship of Ian Elliot who was one of the Vice Chairmen of the Board and Chairman of West Sussex County Council. It went very well and is highly relevant to the present situation about a National Park.

When the Board was constituted there was much talk about the creation of a National Park and the Board was under a duty to consider that possibility on a regular basis. The Board was constituted by an agreement between the thirteen local authorities and the Countryside Commission to last for six years, expiring in 1998. After my first three years I was asked to continue until the end of the six years. I though this a bad idea because new arrangements would be required to operate from then, and it would be much better if my successor who would implement them should negotiate them. So I said I would do two more years and my successor should be appointed at least a year before expiry of present arrangements, and this was agreed.

I was fortunate in getting Tim Renton (Lord Renton of Mount Harry) to succeed me but due to the election he could only start around six months before expiry. I had had long discussions with Richard Simmons who was Chairman of the Countryside Commission on the future and in the end proposals were put forward which were acceptable and came into effect on expiry of the first agreement.

Meantime there was much discussion and conferences were held on whether or not the AONB should be constituted a National Park. Everyone agreed that the Board was a success but there was strong support for a National Park, firstly because there was a statutory obligation on Government to fund it and secondly because it was thought that there would be stronger opposition to development than the Board would impose with the local authorities. I, and the Board, did not agree bearing in mind a National Park was appropriate to wild places like Dartmoor; we were not a wild area and at one point the AONB was only three miles wide. I briefed the Countryside Commission on all this. They agreed with us and, being the statutory advisors to Government, so advised. Long after my time Mr Prescott announced that the area was to be a National Park. I phoned Richard Simmons (who had by then retired) about this the same day and he told me that he had spoken to Richard Wakeford, the Senior Officer at the Countryside Agency (as it had then become) who told him he had no idea Government had decided on the matter or that the announcement was going to be made. I cannot understand how Government can be carried on like this nor why anybody should be a civil servant!

I had given a lot of thought to the possibility of introducing a Bill to reinforce the position of AONBs as to their secure continued existence and finance and had long discussions both with Michael Holdsworth, Clerk to West Sussex County Council, and Richard Simmons. A Bill was later introduced in to the House of Lords by Tim Renton generally on these lines and including provisions relating to planning powers. It was a good Bill but was not enacted. One of my chief concerns about a National Park was that it would have planning powers and there would be endless conflict with neighbouring local authorities. One of my greatest joys was that in the whole of my five years in office we never had a row at the Board – and this was not because we did nothing!

CHAPTER SIX

The House of Lords

I MADE MY MAIDEN SPEECH about a year after my father died. Everyone is terrified of making their maiden speech because one is being scrutinised by a very critical audience who are trying to sum up what they think of the new member. There are rules for making such speeches. They must be short, non-controversial and be on the subject of which the speaker knows something. There is also a rule of the House that, out of courtesy, nobody may leave the Chamber – or enter – while the speech is being made. Having been involved in Refugees and Freedom from Hunger campaigns of the UN through the CBF, I did an enormous amount of research – at Chatham House and elsewhere – on what I thought was going to be the key problem of the remainder of the century, namely the vast increase forecast in population in South East Asia and the migration and feeding problems – and therefore the risks of conflict – to which this would give rise. Judging by current situations this does not seem to have been far out.

A maiden speech is rarely reported in the press and, as to its substance, seems to have very little impact in the House – mine did not! Indeed I found generally speaking in the Chamber a frustrating exercise for a number of reasons. There are a number of conventions binding the House which were introduced to avoid conflict with the Commons. For instance, when the Commons have passed the Second Reading of a Bill this must not be upset by a contrary decision of the Lords. Money Bills may not be voted on (though they may be debated). Restrictions are placed on voting where items have appeared in the Government's Election Manifesto. This seems to me absurd as the manifesto is cobbled together to provide a sufficient common platform for the members of the coalition which forms each party;

it does not in my view show the basis on which they were elected as alleged. Very few electors read the manifesto! I remember when a matter of importance – I think it was Rhodesia – was being debated in the Lords there was a strong view contrary to that taken by the Commons. I think it was Lord Carrington, then Leader of the Opposition (and much respected by all) who was strongly against the Commons view and successfully warned the House against voting in a contrary sense as this 'would create a constitutional crisis'. I wondered why in that case so much time had been spent on the debate.

There is a good practice that one must only speak on subjects one knows about and if you breach this you are likely never to be listened to again. But I found that even if you are listened to, your speech makes little impact as it is not generally reported and Government take little notice if, as is usual, they have already made up their minds. An exception is where one is opening or speaking in a debate on a Report in the preparation of which one has taken part – such as one of the Select Committees – which carry much influence.

Those are reasons why I much preferred to spend time in Committee rather than in the Chamber – educational and amusing though this often is.

I recall two particular occasions when I did (or did not!) intervene in a debate, though I did from time to time and was much encouraged to do so by my old friend Peter Henderson who was Clerk of the Parliaments.

When independence was promised to Uganda and Kenya, the Indian population there were concerned about their future and urged the British Government to offer the possibility of having British nationality so that if, as they feared, the new independent governments treated them badly they could come to the UK. This was promised. When independence was granted to Uganda the British Government resiled from the promise to admit the Indians. I felt extremely angry and I found my name listed twenty-second in the list of speakers in an all-night debate. Of course every point that could be made had been made by then. However at around midnight I recalled some relevant point I had read as a student concerning the law of nationality in Oppenheim on International Law and went to the library where I mentioned this to the librarian. He found it immediately – the librarians there are marvellous! Armed with this tome I re-entered the Chamber and when my turn came spoke. I was cheered on by the five or six members who felt as I did. It had no effect on Government, but I felt I had done what I could and should. Next day in the office I was approached by a very nice Anglo-Indian manager asking what I thought I was doing, attempting to import more Indians, and this was appalling! I gently mentioned that he was hardly a person to complain having been in the same position, but with no effect.

Then there was the Patent Bill which I thought should extend the validity and enforceability of UK patents to the North Sea platforms and oil operations. This amendment was the last and amended the last clause which I had thought would be debated on the second day of the Committee stage of the Bill. The debate went on for many days and I attended all of it to ensure I was there for my amendment. I also looked at the list of amendments put down daily but failed to do so on the last day when mine came up for debate. The clause was called and the Lord Chancellor got up as I was about to do so, and spoke moving an amendment which so far as I could make out did what I wanted. The Chairman (I remember it was Morys Aberdare, brother-in-law of Francis Dashwood, an old friend and client) fixed me with a piercing gaze which told me I should get up and speak. But I was so dumbfounded by the Lord Chancellor's intervention I could not and remained seated. I should of course have got up and said how grateful I was for Government action to take on my amendment.

I became a member of the Consolidation Committee, one of the most boring committees. Our job was to recommend to the House that certain Statutes should be consolidated. This had to be done without changing the law. It was a Joint Committee of Lords and Commons presided over by a Law Lord. Proposals came to us from the Law Commission. A lady who joined us would complain that the law did not make sense and was answered by the Chairman that he agreed, but it had to remain that way otherwise he would be changing the law. That was correct but did not add to the interest of our job.

I remember instances of my intervention largely through boredom.

One related I think to a Solicitors Bill which had passed through all stages in the Lords and had one remaining stage in the Commons. It was proposed that this Bill (which had yet to be passed) should be consolidated. Contrary to the Chairman I thought this was outside our powers and insulting to the Commons who might want in the remaining stage to alter it. I called for a vote – almost unprecedented – and won with support from the Commons members.

Then I spotted that the Law Commission had incorporated Statutory Instruments in the Statutes to be consolidated. The validity of a Statutory Instrument can be attacked on the ground there was no power to make it; a provision in a Statute cannot be. This was taken up with the Law Commission and special provision was made for this.

I did put down amendments to Bills from time to time, particularly to Environment Bills where I knew the subject well from experience on the Royal Commission, and many were accepted. On one Bill the amendments were to come up while I was in Manchester for Philippa's ear operation, so I had to ask friends to do them for me. I never had to ask twice – and I asked members from any party. Of course I gave them notes and they were all proposed. It is this sort of relationship within the House that resulted in its being known as 'the best club in London'! I put forward a lot of amendments to the 1995 Bill, most of which were accepted; they were derived from our long study in the Royal Commission.

But in addition to this I was shocked to find that in this major Environment Bill there was no provision about air pollution. In conjunction with Dr Crossett who was then Secretary of the NSCA (National Society for Clean Air) of which I had been President, I drafted a two-page amendment. Government came back with their own twelve-page amendment much to the same effect which they proposed constitute Part IV of the Bill, to which of course I readily agreed.

I had met Dr Crossett first at St George's Seminar Centre at Windsor Castle which held seminars under a General Beech. It was while there on one occasion that I met Michael Mann who was Dean of Windsor and an old friend of Willie Pybus from wartime days. It was commonly said that he should have been in charge of seminars and Beech (who was a very quiet and religious man) should have been Dean! I had been invited on that occasion to speak on the environmental consequences of electricity privatisation. At first I thought this was a foolish question as there would be none, but the more I thought about it the more I thought there was to be said. The talk went quite well and some of my forecasts were right. I had been there previously, invited to talk on some charity questions.

An old friend from the Regiment had a house within the Castle precincts as a Knight of Windsor. This was Dick Tamplin whose career was in the Army, rather younger than I, who was for many years in charge of the Regimental Museum at Belvoir Castle and made a great contribution as rather a learned historian. I gathered his duties as Knight of Windsor were ceremonial and that he had to do a slow march with the other Knights for regular services in St George's Chapel. When he was struck with Parkinson's Disease there was great concern as to whether he could continue, but with great difficulty he did until he died, leaving his widow who had the same disease. She had to leave the house, but was fixed up with a flat by the powers that be within the Castle precinct. We were together in the Regiment and he gave me a photo of us both at Lamia in Greece which I still have.

When I was invited to join the Select Committee on the EC and its Environment Sub-committee I resigned from Consolidation. The EC Committee had seven Sub-committees dealing with different jobs. The Chairman of the Committee sifted the hundreds of documents received from the EC and decided which matters should be the subject of the Report and by which Sub-committee. Of course there were often instances where the Chairman of a Sub-committee would propose a Report to be made on a subject in his province.

Each Sub-committee had a Clerk. He or she always had a good degree and sometimes a Doctorate and there were mostly quite young – in their twenties when they started. They had a great responsibility in organising the Sub-committee and its work including selection of witnesses, preparation of questions for them (which were sent in advance of the meeting) and writing the Report. Different chairmen intervened differently in all this. I played rather an active part in it all and indeed wrote the first Report for which I was responsible. The Clerk also dealt with all the administrative arrangements.

I became Chairman of the Environment Sub-committee in succession to Gathorne Cranbrook and found that for the first time I was to have a desk. In fact it was half a desk! The Chairmen had a room equipped to take twelve and each shared a desk with another, so there was no privacy and some noise if the telephones were going. No secretarial or other assistance was given and if I had not had all this at the office it would have been quite impossible. We were unpaid like all other members of the House though there was an attendance allowance which rose over the years I was there to £30 per day which theoretically had to be accounted for, for expenses of attendance e.g. taxi fares. There was no place to discuss matters or interview people other than the Chairmen's room itself or the Clerks'. This changed for a short while when I was doing the Murder enquiry so it was then possible to have a private meeting. Prior to that when I was doing a study on disposal of waste at sea I wanted to discuss matters with the deputy head of the US Environment Protection Agency whom I knew slightly. He readily agreed and in my then innocence arranged to meet in the Chairmen's room which we did in the evening in comparative quiet at a large octagonal table. Nevertheless it was not a private room. I asked a secretary to arrange for tea to be served. I had no idea that the resources of the House did not extend so far. She did her best by using the gas ring in her room and serving the tea in a mixture of rather cracked and miscellaneous cups and saucers. Surely no other organisation would stand for this?

The atmosphere in the Chairmen's room was extremely friendly as everywhere else in the House and we all got on very well together. Sharing my desk was Lady (Betty) Lockwood who was Chairman of the Social Affairs Sub-committee. One day as I came in I saw her mopping up her desk which was covered in water and a bucket on the floor beside her catching drips from the ceiling. I asked her what on earth was happening and she said 'Black Rod's flat is immediately above here and he was washing his tights when the telephone rang and he forgot to turn off the tap when he went to answer it'. Accidents can happen even in the best-regulated establishments.

Until my appointment the Clerk of the Environment Sub-committee had been a man whose interest lay not in that, but in translating the mediaeval Latin of St Jerome's letters. Fortunately he left to take a Chair at university to study this! In his place came Mary, then twenty-one, having just taken her degree in English at UCL and the Civil Service Exam. She told me that the Civil Service was not a career on the College list and that the idea had come from a friend of hers.

Our first Report was on titanium dioxide of which I knew nothing – nor did she! I asked a scientist on the Royal Commission who had been head of ICI paint division about this and he gave me a five minute run-down on the whole subject. You could do this on the Royal Commission on Environmental Pollution (RCEP) without embarrassment. I remember on a visit we made that we were staying at a hotel awaiting breakfast in the dining room at 7 a.m. when I said to him, 'You keep telling me about the second law of thermodynamics. What is the first?' and he gave me a civil reply!

In addition to the Clerk we had a specialist adviser expert in the subject. Most of them were academics and gave us excellent advice and sometimes wrote technical parts of the Report. I relied on them to ensure we did not make fools of ourselves. Naturally this being our first Report I took special care in going through the evidence. We had a witness from Greenpeace who produced an aerial photo of the site showing a stain of pollution in a position which struck me as strange. After I had questioned him at some length I asked him outright whether this had been painted in and he had to admit it had been. I felt he should be committed to the Tower for trying to deceive us! I never had that experience again.

Over the years we had a wide variety of subjects to master which was stimulating and educational. On sewage, for instance, we went to Weymouth to see that the outfalls into the Bay had been shifted to west of Portland Bill and that treatment had been applied which relieved the Bay of pollution from which it had suffered for long. We dealt with liability for pollution and rejected proposals made by the Commission with the result that they withdrew them and years later produced an alternative. We went to Spain to see how EC Directives were dealt with in a Federal State. We also looked at the relationship between regional development and environment. For instance one of the special environmental areas is south of Seville, special because of the high water table and the ecological consequences. The regional development programme of the EC involved tobacco-growing immediately outside the area which required much water and lowered the water table! Incidentally, at this time towards the end of my Chairmanship of Environment, my Clerk was Ed Ollard who married my first Clerk, Mary.

We carried out an enquiry into motorcycle noise and I expected that the usual evidence would be given following a meeting of the council of the organisation giving evidence – i.e. that the members were very responsible and reduced noise to the lowest practicable level. This indeed was the evidence first given. Then, refreshingly, the Chairman arrived rather late having been held up by traffic on his way by bike from the West Country. His evidence was given from the heart. He loved his bike and if the noise were reduced it would take half the fun out of riding it! How refreshing it is to have such enthusiastic evidence.

Our Reports were published with the evidence and debated in the House. I regarded it as a high compliment when one of the professorial Peers commented that our Reports were first-class textbooks! The debates were opened by me as Chairman and there were always kind remarks about them. However they rarely had much influence in this country outside the Civil Service where they sometimes tended to mould policy.

The Reports as published were inevitably formidable in size and price as the evidence was usually extensive. Generally I tried to write the Reports in three parts – the nature of the problems, the evidence and our conclusions, the conclusions hopefully flowing inevitably from what had gone on before. On the whole this worked well though obviously in some cases one had to adapt the form of the Report to the subject.

I came to the conclusion that our Reports would be more accessible if published on their own, without the evidence, provided it was made clear that the authentic version incorporated the evidence. I had in mind members of the House and of the Commons as well as the academics and teachers and members of the public generally who might wish to inform themselves of a subject but who were put off by the weight of the full Report, let alone its cost. There was much opposition to the idea, but eventually I was allowed to pursue it. I then found difficulties were put in the way by the publishers so I had them to my office with the publishers of the *Jewish Chronicle*, whom I knew, to advise as expert publishers and eventually it was agreed and done. The resultant short Reports came to be known as 'The Nathan Slim Line'!

After Mary, Tom Mohan became my Clerk, arriving from Westminster School where he had been organist and had played from time to time at Westminster Abbey. While he was with me he was editing an edition of *Palestrina*. How he came to join us I do not know, but one of the Senior Clerks being a clarinettist I believe wanted a really good accompanist! Tom was excellent as a Clerk. Like all of us he knew nothing of the environment and had to pick it all up as he went along – as I did. It was a wonderful educational experience in broadening one's knowledge to have to pick up new subjects and master them quickly.

I had been Chairman for some four years and my last Report had been on the dilution of cadmium in fresh water – than which it is hard to think of a more dreary subject – important though no doubt it was. The Leader of the House, John Belstead, whom of course I knew and who was a friend of Joyce, asked me to see him in his room. He is a serious and charming man. He told me that in the debate on the Criminal Justice Bill then passing through the House there had been a request, which had been agreed, that a Select Committee be formed to report on murder, the mandatory life sentence for murder and the procedures for release on licence of criminals so sentenced. Would I be Chairman? I blotted my copy book with him by replying, 'Murder: now that sounds fun!' as a reaction against cadmium!

Tom became Clerk doing this as well as Environment which had been taken back by Gathorne Cranbrook. We had John Smith as our special adviser, one of the leading academic criminal lawyers and writers from Nottingham, and a delightful man who was later knighted. The Committee was a strong one with Desmond Ackner as a Law Lord expert in criminal law (whom I had known well at the Bar and previously, as his father had been our dentist, and he was at Cambridge with Joyce); David Windlesham and John Harris, both of whom had been Chairman of the Parole Board; Baroness Platt, one of the few women engineers and a member of the Conservative party; and Baroness Ewart-Biggs, the founder of Victim Support which was then a new organisation. There was also Alan Campbell who was a prominent right-wing member of the Conservatives.

At my suggestion Davina Darcy became a member. She was confined to a wheelchair and I had seen her doing combat with the Lord Chancellor on an educational matter in which I thought she had shown much courage. It occurred to me then and proved later that she was prepared to enter cells of prisoners (all murderers) and could extract from them more information because of her condition. She did this at Durham where she was carried up the stairs by the prison officers and spent quite a lot of time with the women prisoners. Indeed we went to Durham because I heard that conditions were so awful that men had been removed to Wakefield and the women sent there. In fact Durham was quite well organised and clean.

At my suggestion we went to a number of prisons, as I had never seen one whereas many of the other members had. We went to Parkhurst where the attackers at the Tory Party Conference were imprisoned and saw them there. I also met a prisoner alone (as I always insisted on doing) and asked him if he was likely to be released. He told me he had been in before for poisoning and had been released on licence to work in a pharmacy! He had offended again and was returned to Parkhurst. But on coming back he had poisoned the Governor's goldfish and that had finished any prospect of release. He offered me a cup of tea which I declined!

Another prisoner I met told me he was in for malicious wounding resulting in death; he had been in before for the same offence. I was sitting opposite alone in the cell and drew back to place my chair clearly between us!

There was a good story of the policeman who called at a house and spoke to the man who answered the door saying he had found the headless body of a woman in the wood opposite; what did he know about it? The man answered that that was his wife. The policeman asked what had he done with her head and he replied, 'I have put it under the stairs out of respect'. I told Philippa I would do no less for her!

We were appointed in July 1988 and I was determined – and said so – that we should conclude at latest by July 1989 which we did. We took an enormous amount of evidence and many people were anxious we should receive theirs. We decided to do little on the definition of murder and not to embark on euthanasia. We concluded (Lady Platt dissenting) that the mandatory life sentence should go as the circumstances of murder were so varied and the judge who decided the case was best equipped to know what was the appropriate sentence. But we made it very clear that the judge might decide on a life sentence in the right case and therefore that we were not 'being soft' on murder. The practice had developed that after pronouncing the mandatory life sentence the judge would recommend the minimum term to be spent in prison (which came to be known as the 'tariff') and that thereafter consideration be given to release on licence depending on an assessment of danger to the public. We were told that the Home Secretary from time to time altered the tariff and were under the impression this was a reduction for compassionate reasons. It slipped out however from one of the Home Office witnesses that in sixty-three per cent of cases the tariff was increased by the Home Secretary. We were very shocked by this which had not previously been publicly known and it was new to Desmond Ackner who might be expected to have been informed. Lady Platt's objection to doing away with the mandatory life sentence was that this marked out murder as a crime of quite special nature. There was therefore a minority Report containing her views which is rare in a Select Committee Report and Tom ensured that we followed the right procedure.

We also spent much time on dealing with release on licence and how decisions should be made about this. We had to consider the European Convention on Human Rights and the Court's decisions on various relevant cases.

In time the Report came up for debate in the House. I had to open it and I was delighted to hear afterwards that Lord Halisham had thought it a good speech. The form of the debate was to propose amendments, containing our recommendations, to the Criminal Justice Bill and the first item was abolition of the mandatory life sentence to which the Government, led by Lord Waddington who was then

Leader of the House, were strongly opposed. I was the teller for the proposition and therefore went into the Lobby to count the votes with my counterpart from the other side. I had never done this before. I must have been nervous because the counting machine in my hand had not worked properly so I thought we had won by a few votes. Luckily the Clerks – and the other Teller – were more efficient and showed that we had won against the Government by nearly a hundred votes, almost unprecedented in recent times. I had to present the result to the Lord Chancellor on the Woolsack and the result was received with much acclamation. This was the situation in which I had to return to my seat to propose the other amendments and I was greatly frustrated. It was only with the help of William Tenby, an old friend, that I found my place, my papers and was able to resume. We won the other amendments fairly easily. It was all a great experience. These amendments were negated in the Commons so nothing came out of all our work. I am confident however that we were right and that one of these days they will be implemented.

While this murder enquiry was going on the NCVO (National Council of Voluntary Organisations) asked me to chair a committee on Efficiency and Effectiveness in the Voluntary Sector. The Chief Executive of the NCVO was Usha Prashar who had much energy and ability. She later became a Member of the Royal Commission on Criminal Justice and a Member of the House of Lords. The members of the Committee were mostly chief executives of Non-Governmental Organisations (NGOs) and we covered quite a lot of useful ground which has been adopted since then. There was much pressure from members to ensure that pressure groups would be encouraged as charities about which I was in considerable doubt. We were in close touch with the Charity Commission and one of our members was Mrs Diane Yeo (wife of Tim Yeo the Minister) who was I think a part-time Commissioner and very good.

Then, with the Murder enquiry complete, I was asked by the Chairman of the EC Committee to chair a special sub-committee created to consider EC proposals for a European Company Statute. We had a powerful Committee including members with experience of large UK companies (such as Lord Aldington) and, for instance, Pirelli who had tried to forge a company with Dunlop at one time.

Lady Turner with great experience of trade unions was also a Member. We found the proposals without much merit in this country as there was unlikely to be any demand and it appeared to be a proposal thought up by some theoretician at the Commission with too little to do. It also contained as a sideline extensive provisions as to worker participation which we felt irrelevant to such a proposal. So we turned it down and it has not reappeared for many years. My Clerk for this was Dr Philippa Tudor, who had married another Clerk who had won the 'Brain of Britain'. I think she would have if he had not! She was a Doctor of Theological History 1495 to 1506 or something of the kind. At the end of the enquiry she and I went to her room to put in amendments to the Report on her computer and she pressed the wrong button and the whole thing came out in Greek. We felt this was entirely appropriate!

She later became Clerk to Lord Aldington who sat at a desk very near me and who became rather a friend. He was chairing a Committee to report on some financial arrangements within the Community, labelled the Delors Plan. Philippa became increasingly depressed as she had to redraft the report continually as the plan was frequently altered and was to be seen walking down the corridor in a very miserable state. Then one day I saw her in the corridor with a spring in her step and enquired what had happened. 'Well,' she said, 'Delors is finished now and we are on to fraud, and I really know where I am'!

Gathorne Cranbrook was appointed Chairman of a Government Commission and had to give up the Environment Committee which I again took over, retiring in 1992.

The great treat about the House of Lords Committees is that they are completely non-political – no one thinks of the party to which any one belongs and matters are argued out on merit which is a real joy. Most members have some special knowledge and therefore a special contribution to make. The EC sub-committees are mostly looking at Commission proposals and there is a time limit, so the technique for dealing with them has to be different from a Royal Commission where thorough and complete enquiry is essential.

Contact between Lords and Commons is sufficient to avoid duplication, but no more than that. I tried to increase it and indeed perhaps to have joint committees partly to avoid witnesses having to give frequent evidence on similar subjects to two bodies, but without any hope of success.

I quite frequently went to Brussels and saw the Director General of DGXI which dealt with the environment. I got to know the legal adviser there, Ludwig Kramer, as a friend and the Director General Brinkhorst who came to Collyers once when on holiday in a racy sports car! They paid a great deal of attention to our reports which had a substantial influence on them. As I have said, the draft on enforcement which we rejected for reasons which we spelt out resulted in its withdrawal and replacement by something which embodied many of our thoughts. So we felt that we were doing something useful.

Towards the end of my time the number of Clerks and the number of sub-committees was reduced in the cause of economy and a decree went forth from the powers that be that Reports must be much shorter and the time spent upon them reduced. We obeyed. I had from the Commission a question as to why the quality of our Reports which had had such an influence upon them – as the only thorough study undertaken – had suddenly so far declined!

After all this time dealing with Committees in the Lords I came to know the Clerks I dealt with pretty well. So I was much touched when the other day, long after my retirement, they asked me to come and have coffee with them in the new Portcullis Building.

After I had retired from the Environment Committee I was asked by Gordon Slynn, one of the Law Lords whom I had met first at the seminar I had arranged at Fontainebleau, to join the Sub-committee on Law and Institutions and found that Lord Hoffman, whom I scarcely knew, was Chairman. It is the only House of Lords Committee which I did not enjoy. Firstly it seemed to take subjects of no importance when there was so much of relevance to deal with. Discussions were very party political and I used to come home and tell Philippa that I really would have to resign from it. Hoffman was replaced by Lord Hope whom I had met in Scotland on the Murder Enquiry and who turned out to be excellent and the tone and mood altered immediately. When I wrote to him to say I was not standing for election as a cross-bencher he sent me a charming reply. (Appendix IV)

For some years I was a Member of the Privileges Committee which meets rarely, but was always interesting. It is the 'senior' committee in the House and I was the cross-bencher, though we never had any party political discussions.

The first case I had was as to the inheritance of the title to which Colin Moynihan laid claim. The previous holder had extensive and curious sexual activities with Philippinos. It was altogether a bizarre story and even the hardiest of us learnt a lot! The hearing went on for some days and we had one of the Philippino ladies give us evidence. Eventually we concluded that the title had properly passed to Colin who is now an active member of the House.

After the Nolan Reports into conduct of MPs there was a review of the same matters in the Lords as a result of which rather different rules were laid down for Peers and these involved a register of interests. We were called upon to consider the mechanisms to be applied – a purely technical and administrative affair. I was a good deal surprised at a subsequent meeting to be faced with questions as to whether they applied to the applicant who said that fees forbidden under the rules to be paid to the applicant were to be diverted to a charity of her choosing. It seemed to indicate a total lack of sensitivity. We decided against her. There was some difference of approach between the older members who did not approve of the new regime and others who did, but in view of the resolution of the House to apply the new rules this did not run.

The third matter was as to the legal validity of the House of Lords Bill (to ban most of the hereditary Peers from the House). The House had resolved that this question be referred to the Committee of Privileges, illegality being contended for by some Scottish Peers and by an ex-Attorney General. There was discussion at the start as to the function of the lay members of the Committee particularly as to their dissent, if it arose, from the opinion of the three Law Lords who were to take the lead on the matter. A number of us, led by Lord Wigoder, a friend from Oxford days and a QC, felt disinclined to be stifled and could see no useful purpose in our membership if we were. Fortunately the problem did not arise as we were unanimous in our conclusions.

There was a four-day hearing with the Attorney General for the

Government and Beloff for the proponents in the English case, and an enormous amount of paper including extracts of constitutional history books going back centuries. The Scottish case likewise took two days and included evidence from academics on constitutional history of Scotland and the Act of Union of 1707. We were all surprised to find there was no Treaty of Union. We decided in both cases that the Bill was legal. Those of us who were hereditary Peers thus voted for our own execution. I felt that the material in this matter and the Colin Moynihan cases were so interesting and unique that I gave them to Sussex University.

I was asked to join the Science and Technology Select Committee. It seemed to me that the subjects chosen for report were all in the research and further education fields in which of course the Members were heavily involved and suggested that they should explore a wider range of subjects so that it might not be said they were feathering their own nest. As a result in the course of a study we considered the future of fuel cells for energy which I found very exciting. We explored the future of fisheries particularly in the North Sea and concluded that the scientific evidence of over-fishing should be given weight and regimes of strict control introduced which Governments were reluctant to do for fear of the fishing industries. We went to Bergen on this enquiry and had an interesting review as to how they dealt with this which was revealing in that they had in place proper and effective supervision where there was none effectively in the EC. Philippa came on this trip.

Then there was an enquiry into cannabis for medicinal use which I found fascinating. We had evidence from sufferers of MS, which I found compelling, that cannabis was the only effective source of relief and that it was grown (legally) in windowboxes to ensure consistency of quality. As it had been used for some seven thousand years as a medicine I felt its use on prescription in proper cases should be permitted without the need to have it go through the Medicines Control procedure which would take some five years and thus delay relief for sufferers. I put the case strongly to the Committee which included several very distinguished doctors and scientists e.g. Lord Winston, Lord Perry, Lord Butterfield (one-time Professor of Medicine at Cambridge) and Lord Porter (Nobel Prize winner) and

I was amazed and gratified to find they agreed with me. We reported that cannabis should be available on prescription and this should not await approval in the normal way for medicines. The Home Office turned down our recommendations before publication so I knew we were right! This Report did however prompt the Home Office to grant a licence for research into cannabis and the growing of it at a secret location which was undertaken by Dr Guy and his company GW Guy PLC. All this led to the proposal that a charitable trust be formed to pursue such research and the first Trustees were Members of the Select Committee including myself. It has now been going for a couple of years with two or three research projects in being. I have now retired as I feel some younger person should come in and I am becoming increasingly out of touch.

I was invited to become a Member of the Foundation for Science and Technology which is very active and of which Jack Butterworth was Chairman – now President – and attend their lecture discussions fairly regularly partly to keep in touch with old friends.

When proposals to revise the composition of the House of Lords came to be implemented I was much pressed by members of all parties to stand for election as a cross-bench Hereditary Peer. A list of the most active Peers over the last year had been published in which my name appeared. However I did not like the changed atmosphere in the House over the past two years or so and I had no confidence in the idea of appointing a Royal Commission with the terms of reference it had to implement the needed changes. I had felt for years that change was needed not least as a result of an experience I had in the dining room. When the House of Lords Bill (to do away with most hereditary Peers) was coming up for debate a lot of backwoodsmen arrived, opposite one of whom I was sitting, a charming elderly man. He asked me my name which I gave and he said, 'I remember your father in 'forty seven. Very good man. Haven't been here since'.

I felt I should not stand for election for many reasons including age. I was getting rather stale with the Committees which I would not in future be asked to Chair, and travel to London from home was becoming a nightmare. I miss friends after some thirty-six years in the House, but otherwise am sure my decision was right.

I was invited, as were many others, to submit evidence to the Royal Commission on the future of the House and I did.

I had a number of amusing and interesting experiences with parties I arranged at the House. It is odd that there are so few facilities for parties there. A European Environment Group was coming over and wanted to be entertained so I thought I would arrange something in the House. In the absence of any other possibility I asked the Chief Opposition Whip, Lord Ponsonby, whether I could use his room to which he readily agreed. This is on the Principal floor. There were to be around fifty guests. I arranged for some canapés and other cold eats and drinks to be available and spoke to Lady (Irene) White about all this. She was a formidable Lady and one of the old hands in the House. She was determined that we should serve hot sausages at the party notwithstanding (as she well knew) that this was forbidden. The only means of cooking was on the ring in the Secretaries' room on the floor above which she arranged with them to use. So this distinguished lady of over eighty years was seen to be smuggling sausages into the Chief Whip's room under cover of a sheet and serving them with aplomb – and great joy. It made her day!

There was the opening of Parliament when I invited a party of the young and arranged for them to use the EC Committee Chairman's room which overlooks Parliament Square and therefore provides a good view of the Queen's arrival; there is a screen there so you can also watch the proceedings in the Chamber. This room is between the Chairmen's room (the one that takes twelve) and the Secretaries'. I provided soft drinks for refreshment, as did those who were in the Chairmen's room. The Secretaries had hard liquor! John Tull who used to drive my car, had driven me up in the Daihatsu wagon which was striking among the diplomatic Daimlers! After the ceremony was over my guests (all five of them) assembled outside and after finding John Tull heaved themselves into the back and front of the wagon and off we went to Chinatown for a feast. It went very well. The guests included Alison Stein, wife of Richard son of Leonard, and her daughter Sarah, and Kate Pybus daughter of Willie and Arabella, daughter of Peter Nathan.

There was an occasion when prior to an opening I was staying at my pad in Kensington where Patrick, our driver, was to pick me up, but he was delayed. On the way to the house (and it was getting very late) we found ourselves behind a car with a five-star general which we followed. The centre gateway at Hyde Park Corner, which so far as I know is never used except by the Queen, was open and the general went through so we followed in hot pursuit. Along the way were crowds cheering and waving to the general and in due course we passed the Life Guards mounted on parade. It seemed to me the only thing to do was to carry the charade off and so in a regal manner I waved to all around! We were never stopped and arrived just on time!

CHAPTER SEVEN

Collyers Farm

IN 1956 WE ACQUIRED COLLYERS, moving from Camden Hill where we had lived for some five years. We found, living in London, that we went for every weekend and holiday to the country where both of us had lived all our lives and the travel as well as the fact of living in London did not appeal to us. We had to look for a long time to find the place we wanted, one requirement being adequate land to house horses and another being good riding country. Collyers at Lickfold filled both roles, but was inadequate in size to house us, and the house and garden were in poor condition. We consulted Bill Turner Lord as an architect to find whether the house could be enlarged to accommodate us and he said it could and we went ahead. A lot of work had to be done which he oversaw and designed while the builders Allfrey's under their old family director did the work and made it blend with the rest of the house so well that Pevsner many years later referred to the gables they had built as 'the Elizabethan gables'!

Lickfold had the benefit of being an outlying backwood of Lodsworth. We had a chapel which was attached to Lodsworth Parish Church which had a harmonium played by our neighbour's wife (Mrs Sharman) every third Sunday when a service was held. When we had a labrador – Salami – he could not bear the sound and would sit outside and howl. When the service was an early one this got us out of bed quickly! The chapel was on common land which I kept mown and tidy. In time the church decided to have it pulled down. This was not too difficult as it was a wooden structure in poor condition. Rupert our son assisted in the demolition. The little 'spire' on the roof came to us and we installed it on our barn in the garden where it still looks well.

Collyers Farm.

At the age of five Rupert, being of an entrepreneurial disposition, took dung we had in sacks round the back doors of houses in the village and demanded sixpence a bag. I had to go round and repay them when I found out about this!

Mrs Dadswell and her son lived in the Old Shop Cottage and when we first arrived the shop was open for sale of biscuits and the like. But the stock was very run down and shortly afterwards the shop closed and the old lady died. Mr Dadswell continued with the newspaper round and came every day in his gumboots from the bottom of which he produced boiled sweets (wrapped!) for the children.

The Lickfold Inn was then called The Three Horse Shoes as it had been for generations. It was owned by a middle-aged couple called Bathgate who ran it as a pub for the locals, and it was used by staff at the ICI establishment up the road. No food was served nor was this then common at pubs. They had a dartboard and I think shove ha'penny and one or two other games and it was quite a social centre. They had a son who was an architect. They decided to convert a corridor into a dining room with settle tables – that is a wooden table with a fixed bench with a fixed wood back on each side. Their son did the design. We went for the opening and they served on family silver and it was very nicely done. However I had great difficulty in getting into the settle bench seat and found it practically impossible to get out afterwards. This was obvious to our hosts the Bathgates. It was then that they admitted that their son had just finished work at the zoo completing the chimpanzee house and the plans had got mixed up.

It was when work was being carried out there many years later that I learnt a tip about keeping trespassers out. They put up a notice saying 'Beware Termites'. It worked!

Some years ago a developer decided to do work on a building long ago used as a cow bower next to a cottage opposite the home used years ago as Cromwell's shooting lodge. He was converting it into a cottage having bought the whole property and selling off the existing cottage thus splitting the property. He had not sought planning permission and Philippa was strongly opposed to the development – as was I. We alerted the District Council to what was happening but they did nothing except assure us that the old cow bower was merely being modernised as such.

Despite our best efforts to get them to act nothing happened until I saw modern loos being delivered and was able to write to the District Council informing them and pointing out that whilst we were very particular in Lickfold about hygiene we had not yet trained our cows to use such loos or indeed any loos! Nothing happened and the house complete with hideous chimney was finished without planning permission. Only when it was complete did they attempt to put an effective enforcement order on and this was denied on appeal.

A more successful exercise related to the new development being made by the local authority in Lodsworth which ended up as the Oakfield Estate. It was very well designed and I understand attracted more than normal funding. It incorporates small 'granny' houses to keep families together. These houses were to be built without chimneys to save expense and to be heated by electricity. Philippa and I thought this was absurd in the depths of the country and the high cost of electric heating would be difficult for tenants.

We learnt of the subsidy which would be available on this electricity which would ease the problem, but we pointed out that the cost of this subsidy would far exceed the cost of a chimney over quite a short period. 'Ah,' they said, 'but that subsidy comes out of a different account from the building cost'. This was so absurd a response that we pressed the point and they decided to build chimneys. I arranged for Lord Ezra, then Chairman of the National Coal Board, to come and open the development which he did bringing with him the Southern Region Manager of the Board. I told him we wanted a fire burning brightly in the grate and surely the Southern Region Manager would have no idea about this. I was wrong. He built a fire fit for a television advertisement fuelled by the latest smokeless fuel! The fires have been much used and few know the story behind them.

I felt when legislation was brought in to enable sitting tenants of council houses to buy them that this was a mistake as the effect would be to reduce the number of council houses available, and to split up the unity of the estate.

The Lodsworth Village Hall had been built shortly after the first War and was on a hill in the centre of the village, difficult to access and with virtually no parking. The electric wiring and fittings were always causing trouble as was the roof and the failure to comply with fire regulations. Philippa had great difficulty about all this when she was Chairman of the Parish Council as had her successors over the years. Its replacement in situ, refurbishment or sale and replacement on the recreation ground was hotly debated and a referendum held in the village as to the course to adopt. Overwhelming support was given to replacement on the recreation ground and a small amount of additional land was acquired from the Cowdray Estate for this purpose. The site of the old hall sold well and generous support within the village and elsewhere made this possible. The hall was very well designed and built and has been an enormous success not least in developing a very active participation in the numerous events and interests in the village. I was asked to open it and we had a great attendance and a band for the occasion.

1977: the author's children at Rupert's wedding.
Nicola, Rupert, Jenny Ruth.

Years previously Government wanted each village to have an emergency committee available in case of need. They had at that time the possibility of nuclear attack in mind. There were then few young people in the village available for this and in the end Tom Reeve (a distinguished engineer long since retired who had played a part in building the Kariba Dam) became Chairman at an advanced age. There was then not a strong community feeling in the village. I felt this suddenly arrived with the fiftieth anniversary of VE Day when the main street was closed and filled with trestle tables groaning with sandwiches, cakes and other good things to eat! It was a lovely day and we had clowns for the children on the green outside the Hollist Arms and everyone enjoyed it enormously. The village suddenly came to life and has maintained its spirit ever since!

The County decided to encourage each Parish to celebrate the Millennium with a Millennium Parish Map. John Fellowes, a professional artist living in the village, took this on and I was asked to be Patron of the project, which I was very happy to do. It was not a purely honorific job as business and financial questions inevitably arose and John was really confining himself to the research for the map and an accompanying book and their production. He did a marvellous job and the original was given to the village and hangs in the new recreation hall. I was asked to launch the map book and we sold many on the night and hope for continuing sales over the years.

At Collyers the garden was in a terrible state and Philippa's father JB started by digging a vegetable garden near the house (where the shrubbery now is). Much time and manpower were required so I organised a digging and beer party and a lot of friends came and had a pint per square yard! The area where the lawn now is was full of horseradish which is notorious for difficulty in removal and had to be cleared away. Derelict shrubs had also to be cleared and the remains of a chicken run. Approach was by a rough chalk track with at the entrance on the garden side a lot of overgrown bamboo which had to be cleared. This was necessary not only horticulturally, but also to make room for the stables which we bought as prefab timber and a tack room. We also bought a cedar double garage, had the concrete apron built and only later put in the drive and tarred and feathered the chalk track as the main entrance drive.

I bought a Howard rotavator with grass-cutting attachment (which operated in front with reciprocating blades) which did us very well for many years and which I eventually gave to Rupert for his garden some twenty years later.

It was a very wet summer and all very hard work, but eventually it came into shape. I used to cut the paddock with the rotavator grass attachment which was a hard task two or three times a year. In time a boy called Cyril who was very strong came to help us and dug a ditch for drainage down the west side of the drive which we subsequently had piped and it has served us well. He also did much work on digging out the pond in the garden for which care was required as the well was at the eastern side of the site we had chosen. From the well ran a pipe to the old kitchen where there clearly had been a pump. There were many rocks in the pond site and thus the rockery was formed as the pond was dug. We found under what became our hay store a huge concrete tank, apparently filled from the gutters on the house, presumably as a further water supply.

By 1959 we were ready to concrete the pond and I consulted Michael Hill, who had been in the Regiment and had become a surveyor, who advised on the rubble to be put in the bottom of the pond and on the concrete required. I hired a concrete mixer for a weekend and was determined to finish the job in that time so as not to incur further expense. Like all novices I put in much more concrete than necessary – a total of fourteen tons! Some thirty-five years later a hairline crack appeared and so I phoned an expert on ponds who had been recommended to me. His wife answered the phone and said he would be delighted to deal with it, but that day was lecturing at Kew! I had had in mind an experienced labourer. However the great man arrived and said the concrete would have to go and be replaced with plastic lining. He sent a man with a pickaxe to get the concrete out and of course made no impression; he had not believed what I had told him about the fourteen tons! So in the end we had the motorway repair drills and huge skips to take the rubble away. I was greatly gratified that the expert approved our original design which he repeated with the new liner.

We looked after the horses ourselves and this was of course quite a labour – which we enjoyed. Mostly we hunted with the Cowdray, but I went occasionally with the Chiddingfold and Leconfield with whom we had hunted from Churt before the war. Even then my father found them very unfriendly and joined the Hampshire Hunt. I certainly found nothing had changed in this respect and Richard Barlow was still Master.

There is a story (which I suspect is true) that one hunting day three members of the hunt were passing through a boggy wood when they saw Richard face-down in a bog having fallen from his horse. They had a committee meeting to decide whether to turn him over or to leave him where he was. Mercy prevailed and they rescued him!

I went out on one occasion with them – as a guest – and galloped across a field in which there was a hidden ditch at the bottom. Most of the Field knew this but one did not and had a nasty fall and lay motionless on the ground as his horse went off to join the others.

Nobody stopped to help the casualty so I thought I should and eventually reached a public telephone and phoned an ambulance which in time came to take him off to hospital. Oddly enough the same happened again on the same day so I again telephoned for an ambulance and the operator said rather angrily that it had gone hours ago. I had to explain that this was a second casualty which they – and I – thought incredible! I found leaving casualties about very unfriendly and was glad I was not one of them!

The Cowdray, whom Philippa knew well having hunted with them for years, was a friendly crowd with a number of farmers as members and indeed one of them was Master. Cowdray was the centre of their country and kennels and stables were there so there were a good many meets fairly close by. As neither we nor most others had horseboxes in those days this was helpful. I regarded Bignor Park or Turkey Island (near Harting) as about my limit for a meet. They were around ten miles from home and therefore about a two-hour hack – and of course home at night. On one occasion I foolishly went to a meet at Funtington near Chichester about fifteen miles away and turned home when we were virtually at Rowlands Castle! I was riding Lulu, a wonderfully strong cob my father had originally had, and we arrived home long after dark having ridden, I suppose, well over forty miles.

Chatham came to Collyers, but was retired and died one hot summer which was sad after all the years we had had him. In time I had to find a new horse and saw one locally advertised whom I went to see and try out. He was magnificent to ride and had a lovely temperament so I bought him and he was a great joy to ride. We called him Conker because of his colour.

On the night of 2 February 1964 we were awoken in the middle of the night by stones being thrown at our window and loud knocking on the front door. The stables were on fire. Poor Conker died and I was very distressed. To start with I thought it might have been caused by anti-hunting maniacs because a number of tyres of hunt followers had been slashed the previous day. However the cause seems to have been an electrical fault as we had electric light in the stables. Since then we have installed a main switch in the house which is always turned off when electricity is not actually being used – and always at night. The planners and builders were marvellous in enabling the stables to be rebuilt in record time – this time from concrete blocks and asbestos roof.

I had a Hanoverian chestnut for a time with a vile temper. Philippa and I went to River Common for a ride when he was new and I said that I was concerned that he went with his head so low. She said this was quite normal for Hanoverians. Next moment I was in the bracken after an enormous buck! He was also very careless. We were coming home from a hunt near Chilgrove, descending a chalky track at a walk and came across a two-branched bough on the track which could have been jumped or indeed stepped over. I pointed it out to the horse who got entangled in it and we all came to the ground. I seem to remember he had his foot in my top hat! He had cut himself badly and in the classic manner I took off my silk stock to bind it up and on my feet slowly walked on homeward leading him. I got rid of him as soon as I could.

Rupert Minor (so called because that was his name on arrival and he had to be distinguished from our Rupert) was a magnificent Suffolk Punch cross-thoroughbred with a wonderful temperament and fully up to weight. He was also quite fast enough for our country. He alas suffered from poor feet and in the end this was his undoing. Then there was Durham – another Hanoverian. By lucky chance I had won a Premium Bond prize of £1,000 and was therefore able to pay far more than I ever had for a horse. Durham was advertised and I found him tied up to an apple tree with a donkey. He was very much a quality horse and a magnificent ride though sometimes a difficult temperament. He was extremely fast and strong and an excellent jumper. Nothing would tire him. I remember Philippa and I were on Exmoor – the old Duke of Beaufort was out that day – and after quite a run with the Stag Hounds we came to a narrow stream bed used as a path to get to the river below. There was a queue and Durham – and Topaz ridden by Philippa – behaved perfectly. In front of us others were crossing the river and some got into a hole under water and walked out – dismounted – soaking wet. We got across safely and then had to cross an ancient stone bridge like Tar Steps. We were proud of our horses and ourselves. We had a very long hack home to Honeymead in the rain and

Durham, the author's Hanoverian hunter.

we arrived absolutely exhausted, but unhurt. When we took the horses to Honeymead we looked after them ourselves so we were busy!

Squire was the last horse I had. He is a grey Irish Draft of just over seventeen hands. When we bought him he had been very well schooled and was a joy to ride. He had a marvellous temperament and was a great joy to children who could do anything with him. Unfortunately he had quite a lot of illness and was often off the road. For instance he was diagnosed as having a paralysed larynx and had to have surgery which took a long time and had to have extensive nursing meantime. It was therefore fortunate that he was so easy to handle. Finally he was diagnosed as having a sliver of bone in his shoulder joint which made him unrideable and therefore he has now been retired for many years.

At Collyers we looked after the horses completely ourselves for the first years and I used to exercise at 6.00 a.m. either on Bexley Hill or in the school we arranged in the field with a floodlight on the end of the barn. Sometimes I would long-rein there which I greatly enjoyed; I was taught this by an old horse coper Mr Lang who helped us with the horses for a time.

Gibbs Cottages came up for sale and we decided to spend the £9,000 required for the purpose in buying them which was a reckless exercise in view of our resources. They had been divided into three, but we had them converted into two cottages in such a way that they could become one quite large house in the future. Mrs Cook came to live in the larger cottage and helped us in the house for many years until she had to retire. She married Joe who had been married before. Sharon was recommended to us by Joe, her grandfather, and has been with us ever since. The other cottage we originally let for short periods sometimes successfully, sometimes not. The village bobby was for many years Bomber Brown who was of the old school, knew everyone and everything that was going on and would look after the gardens of old people if they had to go into hospital. It was he who alerted us to a drugs dealer who had taken the cottage! We rapidly learnt that references were not to be relied on. A bankrupt once came as a tenant after all the usual enquiries indicated all was well!

In time we found a groom who would help with the horses and we had a succession of these with success. As Philippa had become Secretary and subsequently Master of the Cowdray this help was essential. As a very conscientious Master she would stay until the last hound was found and often got home very late and would see to the horse then. Of course the groom helped with exercising. In the early years there was living, in what is now Orchard Cottage across our field, a retired Colonel who had been in charge of Military Police in Berlin after the war. He had had the good fortune to marry the heiress to the Swiss Air fortune! He used quite often to exercise my horse and therefore made it possible for me to go overseas on professional business as I did. He also exercised when I was at home which was a great help.

In due course the Cowdray amalgamated with the Chiddingfold, Leconfield and Philippa remained as Master with Richard Barlow to make an easy transition. Certainly the arrangements for the merger must have been more difficult than a merger of ICI and Dupont!

However, eventually it was achieved and Philippa retired as Master after a year or so.

Meantime in the late sixties I got enthusiastic about sailing having tried it out on holiday with the children near Newton Ferrers and subsequently when we went to Saye in the New Forest. On returning to Chichester I found that the Chichester Yacht Basin had recently been opened and bought from an American for £2,500 a twenty-three foot ply Bermudan sloop called *Pele*. There was Ron Dummer who handled the sale and he was a professional yachtsman mostly delivering yachts. In later years he did this for me taking mine to Kinsale in Ireland, Brest and Flushing so that we could start from there and thus save time in our brief holidays. He taught me to sail *Pele*. She was a lovely boat to sail – very stiff – and had an Evinrude Outboard permanently secured to the stern which worked beautifully.

I found the best way to find crew unless a friend was available, which was rare, was to advertise and I had remarkable replies from people who became close friends over the years. Robin White was very silent and Director of Music and organist at a large school. He had to retire in time as an organist due to arthritis in his hands. He held RYA qualifications of a high order and was a first-class sailor who never flapped. He came on many of my trips. There was Stubby who was in the Parachute Regiment Education Corps whose great joy was free-fall parachute jumping. He would go up the mast without a second thought, but I was glad even he felt sick when changing sails on the foredeck! He and his wife (no sailor) stayed with us at Collyers when she was taken ill sailing with me and had to be collected by Jenny and Nicola from Porchester. They and their daughter stayed with us not long ago and we stayed with them in Brisbane to which they moved as teachers many years ago now, just before the fateful landing at Auckland when Philippa lost her hearing.

In *Pele* I mostly sailed in the Solent which was not too crowded then and because she was so small we could only stay overnight ashore which we did from time to time. The rule of thumb was not to attempt to cross the Channel in any boat less than twenty-five feet so I never made the attempt in her. I did however want to get experience and approached the head of the Chichester sailing school to come on a trip to Poole Harbour and Wareham which he did.

Belle Ecume *sailing up the River Rance.*

Of course I learnt a lot from him. But as we were going up a channel from Poole Harbour we went aground at which he was horrified being then at the helm. He had been captain of a Shell oil tanker as a career so he was not accustomed as I was to going aground. I merely went below, as I did on such occasions which were not infrequent, to brew up and cook a meal!

It was because of the need for something larger that I went to the boat show and decided to buy an Ecume de Mer which I named *Belle Ecume* which was a fast French Bermudan sloop with sleeping for three and an inboard motor – a Couache, part of the Renault stable. The salesman might have been selling a Rolls Royce. We had a demonstration sail from Newhaven and were able to try out everything; I bought her. She sailed beautifully though the height of the cabin caused me some difficulty.

Fairly shortly after I bought her I got hold of an experienced old sailor who admitted to being seventy, but I suspect was far more, to help us sail from Dartmouth to Treguier in North Brittany. We arrived in Dartmouth and there was a gale so we went up this lovely river to Totnes and back and set off the following day across the Channel in a fair wind. This turned into a gale and the seas became quite high, but *Belle Ecume* with storm jib and reefed right down went very well. I thoroughly enjoyed it. Our ancient mariner cheered us on, tacking – very tired by now – up the river to Treguier where we tied up and made our way to the restaurant on the quayside. Our ancient friend who had been so full of activity on the trip now collapsed into the bunk and said he would sleep. While we were dining well the tide went out fast and we took him a good dinner we had ordered and had to lower it by rope to him. This cheered him up a lot!

This experience and his instruction taught me a lot and we went cruising most summers to the Channel Islands, North Brittany, Holland or Ireland in *Belle Ecume* and her successor *Belle Biche*. I had *Belle Ecume* for some six years and then decided I must be my age and get a boat I could stand in and which had a loo conveniently amidships rather than in the bow, as *Belle Ecume* had.

I always insisted for pollution reasons on having a chemical loo rather than one which pumped directly to the sea which I thought unwholesome in harbour! These chemical loos had a tank which was emptied into facilities ashore or if necessary on a long sea cruise, into the sea. In this case you hung over the stern and emptied the tank there. One bright spark on *Belle Ecume* removed the tank onto the foredeck and finding the foresail on the leeside proceeded to empty to windward spraying us all in the cockpit and indeed the whole boat!

Belle Biche was a drop keel Bermudan sloop with legs which I had specially made so that we could go in anywhere and if necessary she would stand up when the tide went out. She was of a class called a STAG built in Emsworth and was twenty-eight feet and rather a caravan, but sailed sufficiently well and was certainly safe. I had difficulty thinking of a name and eventually came to *Belle Biche* meaning 'Beautiful Doe' which seemed suitable for a Stag and in French slang meant 'lovely tart'!

We had adventures in each of these boats. For instance we were sailing off Cornwall during the Fastnet Race in the late 1970s when I heard the weather forecast on the radio of an impending gale and sought refuge in Mousehole. Luckily the tide permitted us to enter and we tied up to the wall. We were wet and cold so I went to the inn on the harbour called the Lobster Pot and asked the lady behind the desk whether we could have a bath (quite a normal request in sailing harbours). The lady looked at her book and said we could have one in an hour. And then she fixed me with a piercing gaze and asked how many of us there were and I replied three. 'Well,' she said, 'if they are all your size you will have to have them one after another'. I was profoundly glad of my size!

Another time we were caught in a gale in St Mawes near Falmouth and I asked the Harbourmaster who was an old fisherman when he thought it would calm down. 'Well,' he said, 'it's coming from the east. Nothing good ever came from the Common Market'!

Flag signals were rarely used, but the Navy sometimes did and when we were entering Weymouth Bay a naval pinnace was patrolling to stop us as there was a practice firing going on. Seeing the flag signal I immediately went below to find out what he was saying. Eventually I discovered it was 'Danger. Desist from your intentions. Stop'. I particularly liked the middle signal!

When we went to Flushing Nicola joined us and was in the cockpit bashing a steak with a wooden post. The Harbourmaster came aboard to collect the dues and commented that he assumed this was the last Harbourmaster. They say the Dutch have no sense of humour!

The great attraction of sailing was the combination of intellectual rigour required for navigation and the physical demands it made. I found navigation fascinating and was particularly proud when we had to cross the Channel from Guernsey in a thick mist with the aid of the direction finder and I told the helmsman to go thirty degrees to port and we would see the Nab Tower off the Isle of Wight in half an hour. We did! One tells of course of one's successes and tries to forget what has gone wrong!

Starting from Brest, Robin White and I and a third man were offered the use of a heavy boat to get around the harbour which had no oars for rowing, but one paddle for sculling from the stern. I had never done this before, but it worked quite well. Our friend tried it early one morning and ricked his back badly. We started off on our trip going south and waited for the tide in a cove just north of the straights through which we had to pass with the tide. We left when the tide turned in our favour and the wind was right for us. The waves were enormous, but not dangerous and we had an invigorating sail to Benodet and then on to Concarneau. There to my astonishment we found on the quayside the Government Chief Whip from the House of Lords. However, the really important matter was to get our friend whose back had not improved to Quimper Airport to fly home, and this we did. Thereafter Robin and I carried on with our holiday and had a very good time. We were of course coming eastward up the Channel on the way home so one sailed with the tide and arrived at the harbours en route as the tide was full and one could enter without difficulty. It is fatal to sail westward because one is either against the tide and can make no progress, or with the west running tide arrive at the harbours when it is impossible to enter for lack of water.

I suppose my favourite place was Ile de Brehat off the river to Lezardrieux because it was always accessible and absolutely quiet and good anchorage. Going up the river to Lezardrieux at night as I did once is a spooky experience as the rocks on the banks cast shadows which look as if you are going into them!

Ireland is an experience all on its own. Approaching from the west one is of course in the Atlantic and the seas are quite large and going up the Kenmare River, which is about twenty-five miles, one does not see another soul. It is very beautiful with the Ring of Kerry and one enters Kenmare at the head of the river in expectation of availability of fuel and food. We found we had to carry fuel (which we needed despite our rare use of the motor) over a mile and in four-gallon cans this is quite a burden! The harbourmasters were mostly English (I know not why) and friendly. They had telephones which I had not seen since the war. You could get the exchange by lifting the receiver and turning a wheel fast to ring the bell the other end and ask for the number provided the operator was on duty, which she was not after 6.00 p.m.

Entrance to harbours is often helped by transit posts or features which you line up on a safe course to enter. This is done in Ireland as elsewhere. What is unusual in Ireland is that right across this entrance fishing nets are laid so that you get caught up in them unless you spot them in time!

By 1987 I had come to the conclusion that my sight was such that I would have to give up sailing which was a great sadness, and so I sold *Belle Biche*.

It was in the following year that Philippa lost her hearing and decided she would have to give up riding. At the same time Squire became disabled as a result of the sliver of bone in his shoulder, and I was advised that this trouble was incurable. I gather an operation might have been worth a try on a two-year-old valuable race horse, but not on Squire. That was not a good time to think of acquiring a new horse and so I gave up riding too.

So the two activities which had kept me sane with a rather hectic professional and public life came to an end.

For the first time since my earliest years I am now full-time at home in my retirement. This is hard on Philippa! They tell me that with increased age one has less energy and resilience and I know this to be true. A wise doctor told me that if you had been active you noticed the decrease in vigour which comes with age whereas the couch potato notices no difference. I am sure I still have energy enough to cause trouble and therefore cast about for new ventures to absorb my interest and keep me out of trouble!

APPENDIX I

Address to Franklin Institute by Lord Nathan Chairman, The Royal Society of Arts on 13th October 1976

I AM GREATLY HONOURED that you should have invited me to address you this evening in this Bicentennial year following such a splendid feast.

A Fellow of the Royal Society of Arts who flourished at the time of the Declaration of Independence – Dr Johnson – expressed himself thus:

> Some people have a foolish way of not minding, or pretending not to mind, what they eat. For my part, I mind my belly very studiously and very carefully, for I look upon it that he who does not mind his belly will hardly mind anything else.

Mr Chairman, in caring for us this evening with your zealous hospitality you have shown that you are of like mind and I thank you for it on my own behalf as well as for my fellow guests.

The excitement and the truth of history lies in the unexpected – the contingent and the unforeseen.

There is scarcely any better example of the play of the contingent and the unforeseen than in the latter half of the eighteenth century following the foundation of the Royal Society of Arts in 1754.

We like to label periods in our history as we like to 'type' people. It is for the future generations to label the mid-twentieth century if they are so rash as to make the attempt. Others have labelled the latter half of the eighteenth century when your great nation was born and our Society came into being as an age primarily of decadent dilettantism of elegant, but ineffectual drawing room small talk. The reason and good manners which were a tradition of the period overlay and obscure the energy and exuberance of individuals both for good and ill – and in many individuals then as before and since, good and ill combined in each – and happily with seriousness, combined with an element of farce and fun. How else could it be that the Rev James Madison, a Fellow of the Society, on his return to Williamsburg following ordination in England in 1775 could go so far as to insist on speaking of Heaven as a Republic rather than a Kingdom?

John Wilkes, you may remember, was thrice elected to Parliament and thrice expelled, elected Lord Mayor of London and thrown into the Tower. Partly this was due to the invective with which he attacked the Government. But partly it was due to other causes.

There lived at West Wycombe in Buckinghamshire an able and eccentric man, Sir Francis Dashwood, who had built for himself in the 1730s an exquisite house in the Palladian style which stands today as one of the great historic monuments of the time. In 1746 he started a club, later known as the Hell-Fire Club, at Medmenham Abbey about six miles away, of whose activities there is no record save the description which has survived by one of the members, Churchill the poet:

> Whilst womanhood in habit of a nun
> At Mednam lies, by backwood monks undone.

Some indication of what went on derives from the story of John Wilkes and the Earl of Sandwich, then First Lord of the Admiralty and one of Wilkes's strongest critics.

Wilkes took down to Medmenham a baboon dressed as the Devil and hid it in a box in the chapel. In the middle of the service (no doubt some form of Black Mass) he let the baboon out which jumped on to the back of Lord Sandwich who, terrified, ran out of the chapel crying, 'Spare me gracious Devil! I am as yet but half a sinner; I have never been as wicked as I intended'.

Sir Francis was at that time (1763) Chancellor of the Exchequer. He became Post Master General in 1766 which he remained until 1781. That was perhaps how he and Franklin first met as Franklin held the same position in America. At any rate they became friends and Franklin was often at West Wycombe which he admired.

Dashwood and Franklin worked together in many fields. They worked on a Prayer Book together, Franklin writing the Preface and Dashwood the rest. Franklin took it to America where it was extensively used in drawing up the Episcopalian Prayer Book. Its purpose was stated to be – and I quote:

> ... to prevent the old and faithful from freezing to death from long sermons in cold churches, to make the service so short as to attract the young and lively and to relieve the well disposed from the infliction of the interminable prayer.

In 1774 a statue of William Penn was erected on a roof at West Wycombe. Franklin advised on the inscription proposing it be shorter and larger so that it might be read from below. That statue, inscribed as proposed by Franklin, stands now in the garden of Pennsylvania Hospital here in Philadelphia.

While Franklin was at West Wycombe in 1770 there was a fire in two rooms, but no general conflagration. The reason was this. A Member of Parliament called Hartley devised in 1755 a system of fire protection involving stretching sheets of tin or copper beneath the floorboards of the first floor of a house. In modern times it was not known that this had been introduced in West Wycombe. It was discovered during restoration in 1964. I suspect that some houses of the period in Philadelphia are similarly protected due to Franklin.

Franklin is said to have labelled himself as 'a miscellaneous man' by which he meant he was interested, active and qualified in a number of disparate fields.

The Royal Society of Arts might justly so describe itself. It came into being to fill a widely felt need to encourage the development of art in its practical applications, industry and commerce. Its short name 'Royal Society of Arts' is misleading specifying as it does only one facet of its activities, important though it is. The full name is 'The Royal Society for the Encouragement of Arts, Manufactures and Commerce'.

At its very first meeting it was resolved to raise a fund by public subscription to grant prizes to be offered for finding cobalt in the kingdom and the cultivation of madder, both being essential for the production of dyestuffs for the textile industry. Textiles had to be sent abroad for dyeing, hence the need. It was practical, strictly commercial and directed to the country's trading requirements. These principles were to be applied consistently in relation to prizes offered by the Society for developments in America and the other colonies as I shall show in a moment and to which Franklin came, as a Fellow of the Society, eventually to object. But to return to the first meeting of the Society. Prizes were also to be offered to boys and girls under sixteen years of age for drawing which 'is absolutely necessary in many employments, trades and manufactures' and its encouragement would be of great utility to the public. Fine Arts were not therefore in the forefront of the minds of the founders. Yet support and development of British painting became an early objective and in 1760 the first public exhibition of paintings and sculptures by British artists ever held took place in the Society's House.

By the award of prizes and medals young artists were encouraged and many painters and sculptors who later gained fame started thus. Nollekins, Lawrence, Millais (at the age of 11) are but examples. By the middle of the nineteenth century, however, partly because of the establishment of the Royal Academy in 1768 which, in a sense stemmed from the Society, and for other reasons, the Society ceased to support the Fine Arts and confined its activity to industrial art which it strongly promotes today. Prizes and medals were likewise granted for inventions mostly in the mechanical field and many came into being as a result, such as a gun harpoon (1772), an electro-magnet (1825), a respirator (1825) and a mobile fire escape in the form of an extensible ladder such as now used (1870).

You may ask who were the supporters in time, money and effort for this bewildering variety of activity. The answer is to be found in the Fellows Lists which read like the Who's Who of the day. Samuel Johnson, the formidable doctor, John Wilkes, Joshua Reynolds (one of the greatest artists), Edward Gibbon (the historian and the author of *The Decline and Fall of the Roman Empire*), Thomas Chippendale, Robert Adam (the great architect who built the Society's House), Horace Walpole, Lord North, William Pitt, Thomas Arne (the composer), David Garrick (the actor), Benjamin Franklin and many others representing every walk of life and every interest. Each undertook to pay £2 2*s.* 0*d.*

But Boswell (Johnson's Boswell) got in by mistake! He was nominated and accepted without his knowledge and was in arrear for three years, thus owing £6 6*s*. 0*d*. 'This,' he wrote, 'was a most alarming piece of news to a man who was trying to calculate a livelihood out of moderate finances. I went and called on Mr Box the collector (admirably named); found him a very civil man'.

He told him he had been in Scotland and asked that his name be struck off and if he came to live in London he be 'admitted a member of that elegant useful and noble Society'! 'I treated him,' he writes, 'with so much complaisance and put the argument so home to him that he agreed to my proposal, and I left him with a cheerful heart at the thought of having six guineas to spend which I had given up for lost ...'

The usefulness and fame of the Society soon spread abroad and like Societies were founded in its image shortly afterwards in Hamburg, in St Petersberg by Empress Catherine and in 1801 by Napoleon. Those in Hamburg and France flourish still.

But the Society, though liberal in its outlook and wishing to share its knowledge with all from any country was concerned with the practical development of Britain. It did not therefore operate abroad, in the King's dominions overseas – that is, the Colonies.

As in England, so in the Colonies, the system of granting prizes to stimulate new products was adopted. There were difficulties enough in England in obtaining expert advice on the subjects for which prizes should be granted and adjudication of the entries. These problems were compounded in the Colonies by distance and inevitable ignorance in London of local conditions. The Society therefore appointed Corresponding Members, living in the Colonies and holding established positions there, to advise and assist them.

Dr Garden of South Carolina was the first. Garden, curiously, was a leading botanist after whom the gardenia was named. He was appointed in 1755, a year after the foundation of the Society. It was no accident that a botanist should be chosen, for the main purpose of the Society was to promote the cultivation of new crops and the development of new species of plant which would on the one hand help the economy of the Colonies and on the other provide a source of supply for Britain.

As early as 1754, just after its foundation, the Society considered a proposal for silk production which matured in 1755 on receipt of reports from Georgia of excellent results achieved there. Olives were tried without success south of the Delaware River but potash production in America was successfully established.

The Society's efforts, though made with the interests of Britain in mind, were successful in assisting the Colonies. Benjamin Franklin became a Fellow in autumn 1755 on his own request to be admitted as a Corresponding Member, and typically of his generosity he sent a gift equivalent to life subscription of twenty guineas although he knew no subscription was required of Corresponding Members.

Perhaps then he was financially better placed than he was in 1770 when, concerned that he would be deprived of his office, he wrote to Dashwood, 'I have enemies, as every public man has. They would be glad to see me deprived of my office. I do not pretend to slight it. Three hundred pounds less would make a very serious difference in my annual income'.

These Colonial activities of the Society were directed by a Standing Committee for Colonies and Trade. During the period 1775 to 1783 many of the Chairmen of this Committee expressed views – or their views may be inferred – on the conflict between Britain and America. One (Lind) explicitly supported the Government in his writings and another (Steele) had issued a pamphlet in 1760 sympathising with American grievances, and wrote in 1778 to Franklin, anonymously, 'a friend that loves, esteems and knows you, as a Man, a Philosopher and a Patriot, but while his country is under the sway of ignorance and malevolence dares not put his name to a mere philosophic letter ...'

Caleb Whitefoord (of whom more anon) lived next door to Franklin in Craven Street and was introduced as a Fellow by him, was sympathetic to the Americans whilst another (Alexander Small) was likewise sympathetic and earned a stern rebuke from Franklin in 1789 who wrote, 'I find by your letters that every man hath patience enough to bear calmly and coolly injuries done other people ... you have perfectly forgiven the Royalists ... I forget who it was said "We are commanded to forgive our enemies, but we are nowhere commanded to forgive our friends".' Two other Chairmen probably held opposing views whilst a third fluctuated in his opinions. The Fellows, then numbering around 1,500 were probably similarly divided. Adam Smith, an opponent of the Navigation System, was elected in 1775. The general confusion was well expressed by Josiah Wedgwood, founder of the great firm of that name (who later became a Fellow) who in 1775 wrote to another Fellow, 'What is it we see in the papers? That the idea of taxing the Colonies is given up on all sides? Is there any truth in this? And if so, what has brought about the mighty revolution? And what have we now to fight for in America? I wish you would unriddle this matter to me. I am all in amazement and know not what to believe'.

As befitted our senior lady member and well known bluestocking, Mrs Montagu, her comment in 1774 was 'America is our child, and a very perverse one'.

Our learned Librarian, Archivist and Historian, Mr D.G.C. Allan, to whom I owe much for his research (and who is blameless of any errors or omission) has analysed the political allegiance of American Fellows over the period 1760–1777, some corresponding and some subscribing members spread over eleven of the thirteen Colonies from New Hampshire to Georgia. Of these sixty-three he has gathered information relating to about one-half and finds that ten supported the revolutionary cause, twenty-four remained loyal to the Crown and one observed a strict neutrality. Thus on both sides of the Atlantic the political attitudes of Fellows were divided.

Franklin himself did not attend the Committee for Colonies and Trade, but did attend the Committees concerned with agriculture and mechanics between 1767 and 18 March 1773, after which there is no record of his attendance.

Franklin and other Americans approved of the work of the Society in the Colonies, at any rate in the early years, but by 1766 Franklin was expressing his disgust at the system of prizes granted by the Society. He was stung into a sharp retort by justification of the British case. 'Why shall I not be permitted,' wrote a British ship owner, 'to buy Pitch, Tar and Turpentine – without which I cannot put my ships to sea; and indigo so useful in many manufactures; why shall I not be permitted to purchase these articles wherever I can, the best in their kind and on the best terms? No, I shall not; for though they are all raw materials, which therefore ought to have been imported duty free, yet I am restrained by heavy duty, almost equal to a prohibition, from purchasing them anywhere but from you.' To which Franklin noted his answer: 'Pitch, Tar and Turpentine used to cost you £5 a barrel when you had them from foreigners who used you ill into the bargain, thinking you could not be without them. You gave a bounty of 5*s.* 0*d.* a barrel to the Colonies and they have brought you such a plenty as to reduce the price to 10*s.* 0*d.* a barrel. Take back your bounties when you please since you upbraid us with them. Buy your indigo, pitch, silk and tobacco where you please and let us buy our manufactures where we please. I fancy we shall be the gainers. I am sick of these forced obligations'.

The War came and went. Peace had to be made. Richard Oswald was Chief Commissioner and Caleb Whitefoord Secretary to the Commissioners – the same Whitefoord neighbour of Franklin whom Franklin introduced to the Society. Oswald took Whitefoord to Paris to see Franklin because of their earlier friendship. Whitefoord wrote in a memorandum in 1782, after he had seen Franklin, 'Dr Franklin having been much teized with people who came to him from London and who afterwards gave unfaithful reports of his conversation, was very unwilling to receive any new acquaintance from England. But at Mr Whitefoord's earnest request and from the high character he gave of Mr Oswald, the Doctor agreed to receive him; and thus the parties being brought together and prepossessed in favour of each other, the negotiation commenced in the most amicable manner . . .'

Whitefoord was in Paris later and his record of a conversation with a Frenchman is a delight:

> He (the Frenchman) talked of the bad policy of going to war with our Colonies. I told him I was *not* the Minister. He said the last Peace we made was a very *bad* one; I replied I thought it was good. He talked of the growing greatness of America, and that the thirteen United States would form the greatest Empire in the world. Yes Sir I replied and they will *all* speak English, every one of 'em. His triumph was checked. He understood what was intended to be conveyed viz that from a similarity of language, manners and religion, that Great Empire would be *English* not French.

In 1783 Whitefoord resumed as Committee Chairman of the Royal Society of Arts.

The first American to be elected as a Corresponding Member in the post-Revolutionary period was John Alexander Hamilton.

Because I have in my address to you this evening dwelt upon the involvement of the Society with America in its first half-century it should not be thought that this was central to its affairs at the time. Its main focus of interest was within Britain and its activities covered an enormous range.

Today our range of interests is no less varied, extended in some directions from what they were and in others constrained.

The constraint arises largely from the development over the past century and more of a great number of institutions and societies devoting themselves to subjects within our scope from which we have withdrawn leaving them to fill the specialised need. It is only necessary to mention the Engineering and Scientific Institutes and Societies formed in the nineteenth century and more recently, to indicate some areas where this has occurred. And so the Society, freed from obligations in some directions, devoted itself to others.

One of our major activities continues to be the encouragement of the young in industrial design. Industry supports us generously with prizes, which last year covered some 25 subjects ranging from leather and fancy goods to cookers and other domestic appliances to television and theatre design. We had some 1,500 entries from around 100 colleges and institutions. Many – too many – of our prize-winners find their way to the U S and Canada where they are well regarded.

We hold some 600,000 examinations a year in about 30 subjects, the majority being in the Secretarial and Office Management fields. A hundred years ago this year we started examinations in Pitman's shorthand to set a standard required in industry and commerce.

We have recently introduced examinations in English as a foreign language, computer operation and foreign shorthand; these new needs arise from immigration, extensions of European (as opposed to Commonwealth) trade, and developing techniques. By our close association with commerce on the one side and education on the other, we act as a bridge to help fulfil the need for standards of attainment by the one and feasibility of introducing courses on the other. The wide spread of the interests and background of our Fellows, of course, greatly assists in this.

But there are other new fields in which we are taking a leading part either because there are no others to fill the need or because we can act as a bridge between those who might otherwise have remained at a perpetual distance.

In 1963, largely at the instigation of our President HRH Prince Philip, we became concerned with the environment, a word which is itself ill-defined, but whose meaning, breadth and importance has become the overwhelming concern of all countries in all continents. Our purpose has been to obtain a general recognition of its vital importance to all, our interdependence regardless of state boundaries and our dependence upon what nature has provided, of which we are but trustees for future generations. That general recognition has come.

Now we are inclined to act as a bridge or forum for those whose activities impinge on the environment. For instance, I was Chairman of a Committee on Energy and the Environment which reported in 1974. This was the first occasion on which those concerned for the environment sat down with experts in energy production and fuel and with economists and others with different backgrounds and experience to consider the topic as a whole. We produced a unanimous report which I still hope may form the basis of Government policy.

Forestry, fish farming, the proposed Channel tunnel and wetlands are subjects we have or shall shortly have discussed in seminars which will be recorded and widely reported and considered. These among others are subjects whose implications are too wide to be encompassed by any specialist society; we try to select subjects requiring multi-disciplinary study and which are likely to be of vital importance rather than, too late, to consider how existing insoluble problems may be solved. Thus we formed the Committee on Energy and the Environment before the Energy Crisis broke in 1973; likewise, our seminar on wetlands was arranged prior to the commencement of the worst drought, as I am told, since the Middle Ages! The conflicting requirements of water supply, ecology, sport, amenity and so forth are nothing new. It is just that nobody has hitherto brought together all those concerned in order to evolve some coherent ideas and alternative policies.

New competitions have been developed recently. Three or four years ago it appeared to us that once professional musicians had finished their training there would be much advantage in the best of them travelling to master classes now becoming prominent, particularly in the United States and in Europe. We are therefore holding competitions and awarding prizes for this purpose in which we have received most generous support from record companies on both sides of the Atlantic, including annual donations from CBS and RCA.

Last year we started a choreography competition, unique so far as I know in the world. A theatre was taken and the dancers from one of our leading companies gave their services free. We shall learn by experience how best to hold these competitions and I hope this will develop year by year.

Each year we have a series of lectures whose purpose again is to stimulate new approaches, new ideas. For instance, we are presently much concerned with genetic conservation – the preservation of plant species from which hybrids may be bred to meet new needs.

This is no new interest as I have indicated concern with the same subject in America 200 and more years ago. Yet new urgency is lent to it not least by the indiscriminate use of weedkillers and the need to increase food production in unfavourable climates and soil conditions.

When I was Chairman of the Cancer Research Campaign I learned what specialisation meant. We have a most distinguished scientific committee to advise. I soon learnt that cancer was not one disease, but many, that there were radiologists, immunologists, epidemiologists, surgeons, specialists in chemotherapy and so forth and that each was so close to a specialist in his own immensely complex field he would not presume to advise on any other. Increasingly within and outside medical science we are having to see with blinkers on, blinkers which are being drawn together fast so that our field of view is rapidly becoming narrower and narrower. Anyone who has used a telescope at sea on a small boat knows how difficult it is to maintain the object in view, each wavelet takes it off the mark. A wider-angle glass alone can be of use.

To reach a right decision, or rather to find the options available for any important matter, I suggest three elements are needed. First, you need people with a broad experience, with their own speciality perhaps; then you need the experts in the fields under review; and finally you need the forum where they can meet. In argument they must be concerned to sharpen swords, not to grind axes.

This, above all, is I believe the part which the RSA can and should play in shedding light on the dimly discerned problems of our times. If we can make the decisions which need to be made in a steady well-diffused light we are more likely to take the right course than if we act in the dark or by one spotlight however bright.

There is no shortage of questions requiring an answer!

Mr Chairman, you and I have much in common, but nothing of greater significance than the memory, the example, the inspiration of Benjamin Franklin. His is the name you bear to your honour and to his.

As you enter our House built for us by the Adam brothers in 1774, you find yourself in our principal reception room – the Benjamin Franklin Room.

A thousand of our Fellows are American; the most distinguished are designated Benjamin Franklin Fellows – and none more distinguished than Professor Simon Lissim, our Vice President in the USA whom I am happy to see here tonight, together with Paul Harbeson our Senior Corresponding Member and his father John Harbeson who has for so long been Honorary Corresponding Member for Pennsylvania and New Jersey.

Once in each year we award a medal for distinguished service to Anglo-American understanding. In alternate years it is awarded to an American and British Citizen.

It is named the Benjamin Franklin Medal. On 6 July this year it was presented here in Philadelphia to W.S. Lewis, the distinguished scholar, on board the Royal Yacht Britannia by our President HRH Prince Philip.

In our history and in our present we share many who have attained greatness. The objects of your Institute and our Society are akin, and we are akin, too, in our inclination to act by stealth; our great achievements are thus too little known.

The Bicentennial is surely the occasion to look back with pride and forward with a firm purpose and to let the world know what we have done and what we intend to achieve.

Our two countries have grown from a common root. Our institutions are moulded by custom and adapt themselves to changing times and needs. Our people are steady with a sure instinct of what is fitting whatever the temporary shifts of fortune.

Our roots run deep like the oak and like it too we have grown long and slowly, and can withstand the winds however strong they blow.

It is the fashion of the age to debunk great men, heroes of the past and the giants of our own day – to denigrate their greatness of mind, of courage and of faith – to make them our equals by pointing to their petty foibles and their minor faults which we all share.

Thus history – and indeed our own times – becomes one great grey cloud lacking those shafts of light, the stillness of the moonbeam and the roaring thunder which are our inheritance from the great, be they philosophers, artists, scientists or statesmen.

Let us honour our past in which so much that is good and useful – and yes, sometimes great – has been achieved and let us honour those who brought these things about.

Let us then elevate our great ones once again and place them on their pedestals.

And I can hear Franklin, whom we share, echoing from his high place the words of our greatest poet:

> Methinks I see in my mind a noble
> and puissant nation rousing herself like a
> strong man after sleep and shaking her
> invincible locks.
> Methinks I see her as an eagle mewing
> her mighty young and kindling her undazzled
> eyes at the full midday beam.

APPENDIX II

The University of Sussex Presentation of the Baron Nathan, FSA, FRSA, FRGS for the degree of Doctor of Laws by Professor D. N. Winch, Pro-Vice-Chancellor (Arts and Social Studies), 21 November, 1988.

Vice-Chancellor,

Ancient rabbinical tradition has it that every scholar should have a trade, that those who are blessed with knowledge or other gifts have a duty to apply them to the benefit of the community. This has certainly been the course in life adopted by Lord Nathan, who, apart from practising his trade – that of an eminent solicitor in the City of London for forty years – had consistently placed his professional and other talents at the service of the various communities to which he belongs. These communities are sometimes local in scope, but increasingly they have become national, European, and now global.

Like his father before him, Lord Nathan became an expert on the law relating to charity and voluntary organisations, serving as the Vice-Chairman of the Goodman Committee on this subject which reported in 1976. But charity was already a personal as well as a professional concern. Hence his Presidency of the Jewish Welfare Board and Chairmanship of the Central British Fund for Jewish Relief and Rehabilitation. Hence too his long-standing work for the British

Empire Cancer Campaign and his Presidency of the International Standing Conference on Philanthropy.

The theme of private means resulting in public benefits, later accompanied by its obverse, the connections between private gain and public loss, runs like a silk thread through Lord Nathan's career, connecting his wide range of interests. It is matched by an uncanny knack of becoming involved at an early stage with issues whose significance to all of us is growing. As the Chairman of the recently appointed House of Lords Select Committee on Murder and Life Imprisonment, however, I can only hope that this is one case where his prescience is at fault.

The Goodman Committee broadened the categories of charity law to encompass benefit to humanity at large by including a range of new organisations concerned with amenity, the quality of life, control of pollution, and the protection of our landscape and architectural heritage. These are all fields in which voluntary organisations have consistently been ahead of governments, and in all such matters, as we shall see, Lord Nathan has taken a leading role. But first a word about a more parochial topic. The plain fact that universities fall within the law relating to charities is now of increasing importance to us as we become more reliant on private funding, and as we are forced to weigh the consequences to our independence of the shift from one type of paymaster to another. As a result of his connections with such learned societies and educational organisations as the Royal Society of Arts and the Royal Geographical Society, Lord Nathan has already given much thought to what most of us have only recently begun to appreciate.

The same is true of his work on energy and the environment. In 1973, before the oil crisis struck and made us all aware of our global dependence on exhaustible energy sources, Lord Nathan took on the Chairmanship of a Working Party on this topic which produced a unanimous report centring on the need for any energy policy to be formulated within a context that was capable of registering its social and environmental consequences. While he had the satisfaction of seeing these ideas accepted by the Standing Commission on Energy and the Environment, he also had the dissatisfaction of seeing the Commission disbanded in 1981. Undaunted, he has found other outlets for his interests as a member of the Royal Commission on Environmental Pollution, as President of the National Society for Clean Air, and more recently as President of the Environmental Law Association.

Lord Nathan does not subscribe to a static preservationist position; the changing environment must be improved, not simply restored or preserved. Similarly with the role of law; he believes that it must play an anticipatory role rather than one that only equips it to conduct postmortems on what are frequently irreversible processes of change – postmortems, it should be noted, which often do not allow a remedy for damage to those parts of the ecosystem which are everybody's and yet nobody's. Law, in his opinion, must not confine itself to the enforcement of existing pollution standards; rather, it should address itself to the promulgation of those future standards which either are, or may be attainable through new technologies. In this way forms of innovation and investment which could minimise environmental damage will be fostered.

With these interests, and as a long-term resident of West Sussex, it is entirely appropriate that since 1987 Lord Nathan has been President of the Sussex Downsmen, the oldest of the county's landscape protection societies, having been founded in 1923. It has largely been through his efforts that the South Downs in West Sussex have been included as an environmentally sensitive area within the measures adopted by the European Economic Community to retire land from agricultural use. If we continue to enjoy the rolling hills within which we nestle, therefore, it will be largely due to the efforts of far-sighted people like Lord Nathan.

Whether as environmentalists, good Europeans, or lawyers, it would be a source of immense satisfaction to this University if we could produce generations of students capable of following Lord Nathan's precept and practice in all respects.

Vice-Chancellor, I ask you to confer the degree of Doctor of Laws, *honoris causa*, on Baron Nathan.

APPENDIX III

'Fencing Our Eden'
The First Garner Law Lecture Speech
given by Lord Nathan
to The UK Environmental Law Association
16 June 1987

I AM HONOURED AND GRATEFUL for the opportunity here in this Great Room to give the first Garner Environmental Law Lecture. I am particularly delighted to give it in this Great Room in the House of the Royal Society of Arts – whose full name is The Royal Society for the Encouragement of Arts, Manufactures and Commerce, having been Chairman of the Society and now being a Vice President.

That the Lecture should be given here is appropriate too, because the Society has played over the last 200 years and more – and still does – such a vigorous and effective role relating to our environment. I am not thinking only of the activities and impact of the Society's Environment Committee, formed in 1970, but also its participation in profound agricultural changes in the latter half of the eighteenth century.

The greatest environmental challenge we are facing at the present time relates to agriculture and the reduction of agricultural production within the EEC. The impact of that policy extends far beyond 'the environment' to its profound economic, social and political consequences.

Great agricultural changes always have profound impacts. In the late eighteenth century the Society, by the inventions and developments it fostered, played its part in creating in many areas the hedgerows and the neat manicured fields whose disappearance in recent years has been the subject of much regret.

But great agricultural changes have not been confined to the last two centuries.

> Forsooth, my lord, quoth I, you sheep that were wont to be so meek and tame and so small eaters, now, I hear say, be become so great devourers and so wild, that they eat up and swallow down the very men themselves. They consume, destroy and devour whole fields, houses and cities. For look in what parts of the realm doth grow the finest and dearest wool, there noblemen and gentlemen, yea and certain abbots ... leave no ground for tillage. They enclose all pastures, they throw down houses, they pluck down towns, and leaving nothing standing, but only the church to be made into a sheep-house ... the husbandmen be thrust out of their own, or else by covin and fraud or by violent oppression they be put besides it, or by wrongs and injuries they be so wearied, that they be compelled to sell all. By one means, therefore, or by other, neither by hook or crook, they must needs depart away, poor silly wretched souls, men, women, husbands wives, fatherless children, widows, woeful mothers with their young babes, and their whole household small in substance and much in number, as husbandry requireth many hands. Away they trudge, I say, out of their known and accustomed houses, finding no place to rest in.[1]

Thus in 1516 Thomas More deplored the radical changes then taking place.

Now once again the fields can scarcely be seen for the sheep which remain free from any Community regime and are displacing both cattle and many arable crops which are in surplus. These are words we have to keep in mind as we face the need to reduce agricultural production.

Environmental benefit from reductions in intensity of farming is now within our grasp; reduction in the use of fertilisers and pesticides, reversing the process of putting land under the plough and uprooting hedgerows will now take place if common sense prevails. Now 'Environmentally Sensitive Areas'[2] are being developed and extended with payment to farmers to help bring these things about, a high percentage of whom have resolved to participate in this voluntary scheme.

That it is voluntary is the key. Compulsion to achieve environmental change by legal sanctions does not work.

Likewise the creation of structures to provide for this is far more likely to result in effective environmental conservation and development than the imposition of penalties by law to prevent, for instance, destruction of forests and the extinction of wild animals. So the first proposition I would place before you in relation to environmental law is that it should be used sparingly in the context of the great issues which face us at the present time.

I first became concerned in environmental matters as Chairman of a working party established by this Society with the Institute of Fuel and the Committee for Environmental Conservation in 1973 to report on 'Energy and the Environment'. We published our Report in 1974 some months after the oil crisis had broken.[3]

The main burden of our Report was that a policy for the development of energy resources must be created in the context of its environmental and social consequences, and that protection of the environment could not be separated from the other objects of a policy for energy. The skirmishing between environmental interests and the energy interests benefited neither side. Our main recommendation was that a Standing Commission on Energy and the Environment be formed. It was formed in 1978. Its Chairman was Lord Flowers. On 8 July 1981 it published its monumental Report on Coal and the Environment.[4] That Commission took as its theme and guideline the main theme of our 1974 Report. On 9 July 1981 (the day after publication of the Report) the Secretary of State announced that the Commission was to fall 'into abeyance'.[5] The death knell had been sounded. It is now dead. It is rare enough to find that a recommendation one has made has been implemented in one's lifetime; it must be nearly unique that it should have been 'dis-implemented' in one's lifetime too!

I have no intention that our recently formed UK Environmental Law Association shall suffer the same fate!

The environment is subject to continual change, part natural, part made by man and the changes may be for better or for worse. The transformation of Romney Marsh to rich farmland for rearing sheep and cattle and the irrigation of barren desert to make it fertile may be contrasted with the desertification of land bereft of trees felled perhaps for heat and housing.

The environment is not wild forests and mountain streams, auks and eagles and hedgerows filled with wildlife and flowers. It comprises all these, but also juggernauts and railways, power stations and coal mines, houses and factories and their processes and products and indeed man himself. Between them all there is constant interplay, constant friction. The task of environmental policy is to reconcile conflicting demands of one upon another in the constantly changing scene. For better or for worse that policy and the way we implement it moulds the world in which we live – our Eden.

In so dynamic a situation the law cannot stay still. The difficulty is and will continue to be to prevent law lagging behind in rapidly developing situations and becoming irrelevant – or worse – a brake on positive development.

Since 1974, when we published our Report, radical changes have come about in the attitudes of industrialists. There is now widespread recognition by most of the importance of taking environmental factors into account. The need to conform to environmental standards is one element of the market requirement and thus offers opportunities for gaining a lead through technological innovation. For several years now this has been accepted within the policies of the CBI as an essential component.

This change of mood is relevant to law and lawyers. Environmental law – perhaps any law – cannot be successfully introduced, applied and enforced unless it conforms to generally accepted ideas, unless it goes 'with the grain'; it needs to form the framework for action; it can never be the spur.

It is now recognised that pollution is one thread in the tangled web of interactions in which we live; it cannot be pulled out and treated, whilst leaving the remainder of the pattern in place undisturbed.

Programmes to develop techniques – and sources – for the production of energy cannot be considered without regard to their consequences. Energy production cannot sensibly be considered disregarding the potential for energy conservation. For energy conservation reduces the need for production and the pollution that creates.

The relevance of the purpose of our Association to these problems and the impacts of the processes of production which at first flush seem remote can most readily be illustrated by waste. Some legal process should be devised under which it is necessary to determine and secure the means for disposal of wastes arising from production *before* it is commenced. The factors relating to the abatement of pollution require consideration at *that* time. The production of energy is one example, another is the production of foods and packaging and the problem of disposal of litter, and then of course there is the production of dangerous chemicals whose disposal should be considered *before* not *after* they are produced.

A question I place before you is how far, if at all, law should be used for 'technology forcing'. If the law prescribes, for instance, standards in relation to products or processes which shall become legally enforceable within a given (reasonable) time this may result in investment in technology to achieve those standards in time – or in elimination of the product or process. More should be made of this technique, an essential feature of which is certainty and consistency of policy. If there is doubt that the standards prescribed will in fact come into force at the time stated there is no incentive to invest. If however there is that certainty the assurance of a market justifies investment.

Best Practicable Means originated in the last century, has enjoyed statutory effect since 1874[6] and was defined in the Clean Air Act 1956. It originated as a means for abating air pollution and its application has now been extended to noise. The definition is as follows:

> 'Practicable' means reasonably practicable having regard, among other things, to local conditions and circumstances, to the financial implications and to the current state of technical knowledge, and 'practicable means' includes the provision and maintenance of plant and the proper use thereof.[7]

Its use has been successful in improving standards by looking at what exists at the relevant time. It does not promote new technology to meet new standards.

How far, I wonder, is Best Practicable Means responsible for our backwardness, as compared with Germany and Japan, in the standards of Clean Air which we demand and the availability from our own resources of products and processes to achieve those standards? For instance, considerable sums are being spent on research into development of pressurised fluid bed combusters of a size suitable for large-scale electricity generation. There is, I understand, some prospect of a successful outcome at or after the turn of the century. If industry carrying out the research had the assurance that standards which their products should be able to achieve would be mandatory by 1995 appropriate levels of investment to achieve those results would be justified. It would surely be far better to invest in that way than in retro-fitting ageing plant with Flue Gas Desulphurisation with the environmental dis-benefits of that technique. The law can play its part in such developments – as it can in holding them back. Openness is a key factor in pollution control. Secrecy causes fear, and fear lies at the root of objections to approved development. So openness, publication and the availability to the public of expert opinions on which to base a balanced judgement are essential. It is just not acceptable for the authorities to adopt a 'we know best' posture, claiming omniscience and dismissing grassroots objections as irrational.

Take, for instance, the release of genetically engineered micro-organisms to the environment. The benefits to be obtained from these techniques are enormous, but so are the risks. So scientific studies must be made on the basis of which rules must be devised for release. The whole process must be open to public debate, but then a further stage is reached, where again publication is required, and that is where a particular project of release is to be undertaken. One comes then to the perennial problems of confidentiality and trade secrets. Is it reasonable and acceptable to industry to require disclosure of the organism to be released – or does this disclosure itself deprive the inventor of all commercial advantage over competitors? Does the public interest require such disclosure so that if not given the release should not be authorised? Is patent protection to the inventor available and does it give adequate protection? If not, can and should patent law be altered so that it does? These are matters troubling all of us who want to see full use made of marvels of science which can be of enormous benefit, but which carry with them potential for disaster.

So the lawyer has to consider whether a patent will be effective to protect the monopoly, whether indeed the present patent law is well adapted to the needs I have indicated; if not whether some other form of monopoly protection would be more appropriate perhaps for a shorter term.

Consideration then has to be given to the situation arising, as I understand, in a recent case before a US Court in respect of an animal to which some element of genetic engineering has been applied. What happens for instance if a pig to outdo all 'natural pigs' has been engineered, immune from common diseases, immeasurably prolific and producing meat of the highest quality? Is this pig patentable? If not is this technique and its consequences to be maintained secret? Some may say it should not be permitted and solve the problem in that way. Is this practical? If not I prefer a 'public pig' to a 'secret pig'!

And yet the economic – and therefore political – power which this patent would vest in the inventor would be formidable. Farmers would own – or rent – their pigs under licence and royalties might be payable for progeny. An independent farming community might cease to exist. These are matters not only for environmental and patent lawyers. They raise issues of great social, economic and political importance. But the lawyer cannot stand aside from them. The lawyer after all is especially experienced in what the law can and cannot do.

Genetic engineering is just one of the fields in which there is no scientific certainty in the present state of knowledge of risks of damage. Those charged with responsibility for the public and protection of the environment may have to act *now* and cannot wait for the rigorous proof properly required by the referee of a scientific journal of the safety or otherwise of a product. The manager has to act, in the absence of certainty, on what it is prudent to assume. The manager must have that power. This may result in the manufacturer of a product finding himself barred from using or selling it and thus suffer substantial financial loss. Guidelines should be established which should govern the exercise in these circumstances of a ban. The magnitude of the damage resulting, the length of time over which this might become apparent, and the widespread effects if the fears expressed proved to be justified might perhaps be the first considerations. The cost of the ban might be measured against the availability of suitable technology to obviate the possibility of danger and the damage which would result.

Such a formulation of course requires to be carefully and fully worked out, but something of this kind should be designed to protect the industrialist against the capricious use by authority of the power to ban which should be vested in it.

It is evident that as environmental considerations are integrated into all activity the lawyer will be increasingly involved in formulation of appropriate laws and regulations, in effective and sensible enforcement and in protection from abuse by those in authority.

And this brings one to the question of compensation for damage caused for instance by a defective product or process. Civil – or for that matter criminal – law generally relates to damage to the person or property. It is this which gives rise to special problems in relation to protection of the environment where that which is damaged may not be property capable, as a matter of law, of being reduced into ownership.

For instance, the new Consumer Protection Act[8] provides for product liability in respect of death or personal injury or any loss or damage to any property caused by a defect in a product. There are many exceptions and qualifications, but that is the essence of what the Act seeks to do. It seems clear that no liability under the Act could arise in respect of a defect in a product causing the death of wild birds or fish or perhaps any fauna making up the aquatic ecosystem of a lake or river which are incapable of being the subject of ownership. This would apply I suggest to damage caused by a genetically engineered micro-organism released to the environment as much as to any other product, for there is at least a strong argument that such an organism is 'a product' for the purposes of the Act.

And if release of such organisms which (whether due to a defect or not) kills or injures protected species of wild birds or bats or insects – or amoeba – difficult questions, as it seems to me, arise as to whether anyone can claim for the resulting damage.

And it is this which brings one to consider whether Criminal Law could be applied to provide compensation. An attempt was made in the Oil Pollution Act 1971 which created criminal liability with fines of up to £50,000 for oil pollution offences. There were special and unusual provisions under which the court might order all or part of the fine to be paid for defraying the cost of removal of oil or making good damage attributable to the offence.

But the Courts have established in accordance with generally accepted principles of criminal law that no element of compensation should enter the *assessment of the amount* of a fine. So that route is closed.

It has always struck me as odd that destruction of the very basis of our existence, the ecosystems upon which we all depend – or indeed of the breeding grounds of Dover sole (which, alas is not my only source of food!) – can rarely be the subject of compensation.

The point came to me with particular force when, in June 1979, a ship of some 1785 DWT called Tarpenbek collided with the Sir Geraint off Selsey Bill. The Tarpenbek was a small oil product tanker carrying lubricating oil. The cargo tanks were not ruptured, but the ship was severely damaged and she capsized with virtually no oil spillage. The state of wind, sea and tide made it dangerous to life to attempt to transfer the oil cargo; any spillage would have severely affected fishery, ecological and amenity interests at Selsey Bill itself (where inshore are the nursery grounds for much of the sole found in the Channel), Pagham, Chichester and Langston Harbours which are conservation centres (particularly as bird sanctuaries) and of course popular beaches in the area.

The Tarpenbek, capsized as she was, was towed to Sandown Bay as a safe haven and there the oil was pumped out while she was inverted without oil spillage. After some difficulty she was turned upright (parbuckled is I believe the technical term) and, to guard against the possibility of oil spillage, two small aircraft equipped to spray any oil that did escape flew overhead. One of these, alas, crashed into the sea below Culver Cliff; the pilot jumped out and swam ashore, the pollution from this crash fortunately dispersed quickly. I was there. I sailed out with my godson, then aged ten to see this remarkable operation. We had quite a day! I cooked curry for us all on the way back to Chichester. On being asked by his mother on our return whether he had had an interesting day he replied, 'Yes, I had a marvellous curry lunch'. Such is the impact on the young of great feats to save the environment!

It was however this experience which brought to my mind that had a serious oil or chemical spill taken place off Selsey Bill, areas enjoyed by a great number and variety of people who came specially to visit them as well indeed as those who live locally would have been severely damaged. Such losses will rarely be quantifiable in terms of money. Yet there is no doubt that loss would have been suffered by the community. The problem of qualification of damage could be resolved by analogy with claims for general as contrasted with special damages in claims for personal injury or libel.

I suggest that it is wrong that a community which suffers damage of this kind – it may indeed be destroyed – should be without any remedy. A similar problem arises for instance when an ecosystem in a river, or indeed in coastal waters – and perhaps beyond – has been severely damaged or destroyed, but is not confined to such instances. And yet the mounting of such a claim under our present law will often be impossible.

One of the instances in which these problems were addressed was in the case of the Zoe Colcotroni, which first came before the District Court of Puerto Rico in 1978.[9]

The vessel ran aground off Puerto Rico. Having failed to rock the vessel free, the Master lightened his ship by dumping over 5,000 tons of crude oil into the sea. The resultant slick inundated the Puerto Rican Bay causing great environmental damage including destruction of flora and fauna.

The Court held that the Commonwealth of Puerto Rico had standing to sue and recover damages for harm to its bay and related resources.

As to the measure of damages, an expert calculated the loss of 1,138 creatures per square metre, leading to an estimate of 92,109,720 creatures destroyed by the oil. Monetary damages were then calculated by reference to ecological supply catalogues. Total replacement value was assessed at $5,526,583 or an average replacement value was 6 cents per creature destroyed.

Mr Chairman, I am not making this up! I derive much of this material from a Report of the Advisory Committee on Pollution of the Sea on the Concept and Scope of Compensable Damage caused by Marine Oil Pollution with Special Reference to Environmental

Damage[10] prepared in 1981 as well, of course, as the official reports of the cases.

You will be glad to know that in the Court of Appeals the Court[11] concluded – and I quote:

> To say that the law on this question is unsettled is vastly to understate the situation. The parties in this lawsuit and we ourselves, have ventured far in uncharted waters.

I suggest it is high time we ventured forth into these uncharted waters, perhaps with the Attorney General at the helm acting for the Queen as *parens patriae*. He could perhaps act in a capacity similar to that which he is bound to do for the objects of charitable trusts. Or maybe there should be legislation. To sit back supine and accept as we appear to now, that, in general, damage to ecosystems on which we all depend for our existence, cannot give rise to claims for compensation is not an acceptable option.

The United States have adopted the legislative route, establishing the right of specified public authorities to sue, defining the damage in respect of which a suit can be brought and by regulation, the measure of damage which may be claimed and the application of damages recovered. This legislation with its most recent amendments and regulations seems now to be complete and finalised in March 1987.[12] We should consider it urgently.

Environmental law often involves the creation of offences. For what that law protects often is ecology or ecosystems – the world in which we live.

The creation of offences with a view to the protection of human health may have, as an unexpected consequence, adverse environmental effects. For instance, there was the case of the caterpillar in the tin of peas. Under the Food and Drugs Act 1955 it is an offence to sell food not of the nature, substance or quality demanded by the purchaser. A defence is allowed if the defendant can prove that the presence of some foreign matter was an *unavoidable* consequence of the process of collection or preparation of the food; it is not enough for the defendant to show that he took all reasonable precautions.

There has been much worry about excessive use in agriculture and horticulture of pesticides and other chemicals, encouraged by food processors as an insurance against the presence of insects and thus against prosecution. That is why the recommendation was made that pesticide usage should be reduced to the minimum consistent with efficient food production and that the Food and Drugs Act should be amended to give effect to this – to enlarge the available defences.

The case came before the House of Lords who were critical that a prosecution had been commenced at all. The Lord Chancellor tells the story in his judgement from which I quote briefly.

> When Mrs Voss got home she discovered that the tin, in addition to something more than 150 peas, contained a green caterpillar, the larva of one of the species of hawk moth. This innocent insect, thus deprived of its natural destiny, was in fact entirely harmless ... and had she cared to do so Mrs Voss could have consumed the caterpillar without injury to herself and even, perhaps, with benefit. She was not however to know this and with commendable civic zeal she felt it her duty to report the matter to the local authority and in consequence, grinding slow, but exceeding small, the machinery of the law was set in inexorable motion.
>
> Thereafter the caterpillar achieved a sort of posthumous apotheosis. From local authority to the Dorchester magistrates, from the Dorchester magistrates to a Divisional Court presided over by the Lord Chief Justice of England, from the Lord Chief Justice to the House of Lords, the immolated insect has at length plodded its methodical way to the highest tribunal in the land.

We spend much time on the intricacies of the law, the disputes and differences of approach within the European Communities, indeed within the larger international community. I have today ignored these. I have cast the net wide, for I believe that the interests of our Association should not be confined.

I have touched on a number of matters which have, over the years, intrigued or vexed me. I have asked questions rather than sought answers. I hope that over the coming months and years you, our members and friends, expert in so many aspects of environment and the law, may find those answers.

I shall have achieved my purpose in this first Garner Lecture if somewhere between the devouring sheep of Thomas More and the Lord Chancellor's immolated insect I have stimulated an interest in how best we may erect a fence about our Eden.

References

1. *Utopia*, Thomas More (1516), as quoted in *The Transformation of Medieval England 1370–1529*, John A.T. Thomson (Longmans, 1983), p. 40.
2. See S.13, Agriculture Act, 1986.
3. *Energy and the Environment* (1974). Report of a working party set up jointly by the Committee for Environmental Conservation, Royal Society of Arts, and Institute for Fuel (Royal Society of Arts, London).
4. Commission for Energy and the Environment (1981), *Coal and the Environment* (HMSO, London).
5. *Hansard*, House of Commons, 9 July 1981. Written Answer Col. 216.
6. Alkali Act, 1874.
7. Clean Air Act, 1956 S. 34 (1).
8. Consumer Protection Act 1987.
9. Commonwealth of Puerto Rico *v* Zoe Colcotroni (1978), 46 F. Supp. 1327, US D.C.D. Puerto Rico, 29 August 1978.
10. Report by P. Birnie, F.D. Brown, M. Bruce, Lady Kennet, Mme Remond-Gouilloud and Dr V. Shebek (December 1981, finalised August 1983), addressed to the Commission of the European Communities.
11. Puerto Rican App (1979) Court 628 Fed. Rep. 2nd Series 652 CA First Circuit, 12 August 1980.
12. The Comprehensive Environmental Response, Compensation and Liability Act of 1980 (Superfund) (PL96-510) as amended by The Superfund Amendments and Re-authorisation Act of 1986 (PL 99-499) and the Natural Resource Damage Assessments rules (Federal Register Vol. 51, No. 148, 1 August 1986) (Federal Register Vol. 52 No. 54, 20 March 1987).

APPENDIX IV

The Right Honourable the Lord Hope of Craighead

The Rt Hon the Lord Nathan
House of Lords
London SW1A 0PW

29 October 1999

Dear Lord Nathan,

Thank you so much for your letter of 25 October 1999 in which you told me that you had come to the view that, as you had decided not to put yourself forward for election as an Hereditary Peer, you should not attend any further meetings of Sub-Committee E.

It is a tribute to the part which you have played in our proceedings and the great affection in which you are held by all members of the Sub-Committee that there was a chorus of regret from everyone present when I told them at our meeting this week of the decision which you have taken and passed on your very kind words of good wishes. There was, of course, a full understanding of the reasons which have led you to take this course and much sadness that matters have turned out this way. But there was a great sense of affection for you and for what you have done for us which was, I think, quite out of the ordinary.

For my own part, I am particularly grateful for the support and encouragement which you have given to me during my Chairmanship. The work of the Sub-Committee is as demanding as it is interesting. I have always been conscious of the burden which it imposes on all members, without whose support it would be impossible to achieve the great volume of business which we get through each term. Your unique combination of experience, common sense and good humour has contributed so much to our discussions, and it will be greatly missed.

I send you warmest thanks and good wishes from us all.

Yours ever,

David.

Law Lords Corridor, House of Lords, London SW1A 0PW
Tel: 0171 219 3202 Fax: 0171 219 6156

Index

Italic entries refer to pictures